D0991847

The Nature and Functions of Dreaming

Other Books by Ernest Hartmann

The Biology of Dreaming

Adolescents in a Mental Hospital
(with Betty Glasser, Milton Greenblatt,
Maida H. Solomon, and Daniel Levinson)

Boundaries in the Mind

The Functions of Sleep

The Nightmare

The Sleep Book

Sleep and Dreaming, Editor

The Sleeping Pill

Dreams and Nightmares: The Origin and Meaning of Dreams

Boundaries: A New Way to Look at the World

The Nature and Functions of Dreaming

Ernest Hartmann, M.D.

OXFORD
UNIVERSITY PRESS
2011

10/25/11
Lan
$39.95

OXFORD
UNIVERSITY PRESS

Oxford University Press, Inc., publishes works that further
Oxford University's objective of excellence in research,
scholarship, and education.

Oxford New York
Auckland Cape Town Dar es Salaam Hong Kong Karachi
Kuala Lumpur Madrid Melbourne Mexico City Nairobi
New Delhi Shanghai Taipei Toronto

With offices in
Argentina Austria Brazil Chile Czech Republic France Greece
Guatemala Hungary Italy Japan Poland Portugal Singapore
South Korea Switzerland Thailand Turkey Ukraine Vietnam

Copyright © 2011 by Oxford University Press, Inc.

Published by Oxford University Press, Inc.
198 Madison Avenue, New York, New York 10016

www.oup.com

Oxford is a registered trademark of Oxford University Press, Inc.

All rights reserved. No part of this publication may be reproduced, stored in a retrieval system, or transmitted, in any form or by any means, electronic, mechanical, photocopying, recording, or otherwise, without the prior permission of Oxford University Press

Library of Congress Cataloging-in-Publication Data

Hartmann, Ernest, 1934-
The nature and functions of dreaming / by Ernest Hartmann.
p. cm.
Includes bibliographical references and index.
ISBN 978-0-19-975177-8
1. Dreams. 2. Dream interpretation. I. Title.
BF1091.H3657 2010
154.6'3–dc22 2010009156

ISBN-13: 978-0-19-975177-8
ISBN-10: 0-19-975177-3

9 8 7 6 5 4 3 2 1
Printed in the United States of America on acid-free paper

Contents

The Nature and Functions of Dreaming

1 Introduction. Overview of the Contemporary Theory of Dreaming

APPROACHES TO DREAMING. DEVELOPMENT OF THE CONTEMPORARY THEORY. FROM THE TIDAL WAVE DREAM TO THE NATURE AND FUNCTIONS OF DREAMING

I have been fascinated by dreams for many years (for almost my entire life in fact); my own dreams, my patients' dreams, and the biology and psychology of dreaming. My collaborators and I have studied dreams from numerous points of view. This book is an attempt to put together my work, and that of many others, into one coherent theory.

One starting point was the biology of dreaming, or rather the biology of REM (rapid eye movement) sleep. The discovery of REM sleep in the 1950s (Aserinsky and Kleitman 1953) was tremendously exciting. A great deal of my work in the 1960s and 70s helped to delineate the characteristics of REM sleep. REM sleep turns out to be an organismic state—a state of the entire body—during which everything in the brain and body is controlled and regulated in a way that is different from the regulation that occurs in waking or in NREM (non-rapid eye movement) sleep. My collaborators and I demonstrated, for instance, that the REM-NREM cycle is a basic cycle of the mammalian body, similar to the pulse cycle or the respiratory cycle (Hartmann 1967, 1968). For a time we believed that understanding REM sleep was equivalent to understanding dreaming, since most or all dreams seemed to occur during REM sleep. Now things are not so simple. I would summarize our current views by saying REM sleep is the best, but not the only, place to find a dream. The cortical activation patterns, which underlie dreaming, occur regularly during REM but can occur at other times as well.

Studies of REM and NREM sleep have been invaluable in our understanding of sleep and waking in general and our diagnosis and treatment of many sleep-related illnesses. Human knowledge progresses in mysterious ways. The great interest in REM and NREM sleep in the 1960s and 70s was fueled by interest in dreaming. It was hoped that this work would soon lead to a complete understanding of the nature of dreaming and of psychosis, which was always considered closely linked to dreaming—a "waking dream." This did not happen. However, this work on sleep did lead to an entirely new field of medicine, now known as sleep medicine, which has helped thousands of patients with conditions such as obstructive sleep apnea and narcolepsy. This is a field not even dreamt of by the early REM researchers.

Recent brain imaging studies have added even more details about the biology of REM sleep. However, these studies do not tell us much about the dream itself. We do not yet have a methodology to study the biology of dreams that may occur in NREM sleep or at sleep onset, or dreams we may have during quiet waking states. And even in REM sleep these studies give us only the background biology and cannot tell us anything about when the dream is occurring or what kind of dreaming is occurring. So, studying REM sleep has been useful and exciting, but it has not answered the basic questions of the nature and functions of dreaming.

In addition to my research on REM sleep, I have devoted years to helping people in psychotherapy, as a psychoanalyst and psychotherapist, and this has involved working with patients' dreams. Along the way I also wrote down all my own dreams whenever I remembered them, and tried to work on them and make sense of them whenever I had the time. This process convinced me that dreams can certainly be helpful in understanding what is going on in a patient's mind, or in our own minds. (I agree fully with one of Freud's best-known views, usually summarized as: "The dream is the royal road to the unconscious." But I disagree with Freud's even better known statement, "Every dream, when fully understood, is the fulfillment of a wish.") Still, all this important work on understanding patients' dreams and our own dreams does not tell us what a dream *is*, or what its adaptive functions, if any, may be.

I will try here to answer the basic questions on the nature and functions of dreaming. In other words, what is dreaming and what, if anything, is it good for? Much of this book will be devoted to exploring these questions, based on many avenues of research followed by my collaborators and myself, and by numerous others. I will start with the "tidal wave dream," since it is central to the theory. An adult, soon after a major trauma of any kind, often dreams: "... and then a huge wave comes and sweeps me away. I struggle... wake up." Such dreams are paradigmatic, because they so clearly reflect the patient's emotional state. The dreamer does not dream about the actual event (the fire, rape, attack). Rather, s/he pictures the emotion—I feel terrified, I feel overwhelmed. So in the simplest case, the powerful Central Image of the dream pictures the powerful underlying emotion.

That was our starting point, and I'll start with it in Chapter 1. Here in brief, are our main conclusions, which give us in outline form the Contemporary Theory of Dreaming. Each point will be explained and presented in detail in later chapters.

1) Dreaming is a form of mental functioning. It is not an alien intrusion, not material in a foreign language, and not separable from our other mental functioning. It is one end of a continuum of mental functioning (which means chiefly cerebral cortical functioning) running from focused waking thought at one end, through fantasy, daydreaming, and reverie, to dreaming at the other end.

2) Dreaming is hyper-connective. At the dreaming end of the continuum connections are made more easily than in waking, and connections are made more broadly and loosely. Dreaming avoids tightly structured, overlearned material. We do not dream of the three *R*'s. Dreaming always involves new connections; dreaming is creation, not replay.

3) The connections are not made randomly. They are guided by the emotions of the dreamer. The dream, and especially the Central Image of the dream, pictures or expresses the dreamer's emotion or emotional concerns. The more powerful the emotion, the more powerful (intense) is the Central Image.

4) The form or "language" of dreams is mainly picture-metaphor. But this is not a language restricted to dreaming. It is the way things are expressed towards the right-hand end of the continuum. At this end of the continuum there is less serial processing, less task-orientation, less functioning by formal rules, less constraint. The system "relaxes" into a default mode, functioning by similarity (metaphor), rather than formal rules, guided by whatever emotions or emotional concerns are present.

5) Functions of dreaming. This making of broad connections guided by emotion has an adaptive function, which we conceptualize as "weaving in" new material—taking new experiences and gradually connecting them, integrating them, into existing memory systems. In other words, the dream helps us to build and rebuild a meaningful emotional memory system, which is the basis of our individual selves. This primary function occurs whether or not a dream is remembered. When a dream is remembered, the broad connections can also be adaptive in increasing self-knowledge and producing new insights and creations.

6) Function of the continuum. In addition to the functions of dreaming (above), the entire focused waking-to-dreaming continuum has an adaptive function. It is obviously useful for us to be able to think in direct, focused, serial fashion at certain times, and at other times to associate more broadly, and loosely—in other words, to daydream and to dream.

2 The Tidal Wave Dream

The tidal wave dream, after a trauma, is paradigmatic. The Central Image of the dream pictures the emotion of the dreamer. This is the simplest case, when there is a single overwhelming emotion.

Rather than examining the points of the contemporary theory in numerical order, I would like to start this discussion with a dream—the tidal wave dream—which leads us straight into the heart of the theory. And indeed, a major part of our research began with this dream—a dream that lets us see especially clearly what is going on in all dreaming. The tidal wave dream, and its many variants, is a dream which we have found to occur frequently after a traumatic event of any kind, such as an escape from a burning house, a severe accident, a rape, or an attack.

> *I am walking along the beach. I think someone is with me, maybe my friend K. Suddenly a huge wave thirty feet tall comes and sweeps us away. I am under water struggling to get to the surface when I wake up.*

I consider this dream to be extremely important because it is a paradigm. In this dream, and similar dreams, it is obvious what is going on. The dreamer quoted above was a man who had recently escaped from a burning house in which a member of his family had died. He lived hundreds of miles from the ocean, and had not been near the ocean for at least a year. Clearly, the dream is not picturing what actually happened recently in his life. The dream is picturing his emotion: "I am terrified. I am overwhelmed. I am vulnerable."

We have seen the tidal wave dream and similar dreams after many kinds of trauma, including accidents, natural disasters such as forest fires or earthquakes, and man-made disasters including rapes, attacks, and the death of a buddy on the battlefield. Similar tidal wave dreams have been reported by others, for instance Alan Siegel (1996) in survivors of the Oakland-Berkeley fires of 1991. The dream includes an intense powerful image that appears to picture a powerful, overwhelming emotion in the dreamer: I am terrified, I am vulnerable.

The image does not have to be literally a tidal wave. There are many other ways of picturing the same emotions. Here are some examples from dreams we have collected, which seem to picture the basic emotion of terror or fear:

A whirlwind carries me away.

A house is burning and no one can get out.

A gang of evil men, Nazis maybe, are chasing me.

Here are a few examples that appear to picture helplessness and vulnerability

I dreamt about children, dolls — dolls and babies all drowning.

He skinned me and threw me in a heap with my sisters; I could feel the pain, I could feel everything.

I saw a small hurt animal lying in the road, bleeding.

Other powerful emotions are pictured as well. Here are some images portraying guilt—survivor guilt or feeling guilty about not being able to do enough.

A shell heads for us (just the way it really did) and blows up, but I can't tell whether it's me or my buddy Jack who is blown up.

I let my children play by themselves and they get run over by a car.

My little girl is in a strange house somewhere and I can't find her.

Here are some dream images clearly portraying a feeling of loss or sadness. Each of these occurred soon after the sudden death of the dreamer's mother:

A mountain has split. A large hill or mountain has split into two pieces, and there are arrangements I have to make to take care of it.

A huge tree has fallen down right in front of us.

I'm in this huge barren empty space. There are ashes strewn all about.

At least in these very straightforward situations it appears that the emotion of the dreamer is being directly pictured by the dream or by the powerful Central Image of the dream. The idea that the imagery of the dream is influenced by the underlying emotion is one of the central points of the Contemporary Theory of Dreaming. In the clearest cases, such as those illustrated above, the dream image actually pictures the emotion.

Of course, these cases are extreme examples. In a more average dream things are not so straightforward. It sometimes appears that a great deal of material is being thrown together without any obvious picturing of emotion. I believe that the tidal wave dream and its many variants occur in the unusual situation when there is one overwhelming emotion. Usually this is not the case. There may be several emotions or emotional concerns present, with no one of them totally dominant. The theory suggests in general that dreams make connections broadly among material in the memory systems, guided by the emotion of the dreamer. Only in the case where there is a single strong emotion that eclipses everything else does something like the tidal wave dream emerge. A great deal of our research, to be discussed in the next chapter, shows that the underlying emotion influences the imagery of the dream, and that the power of the Central Image is a measure of the strength of the emotion.

3 Emotion Guides the Dream. The Central Image of the Dream Pictures and Measures the Emotion

Many research studies are presented, demonstrating that the dream is guided by the emotions of the dreamer. The dream, and especially the Central Image of the dream, pictures ("contextualizes") the dreamer's emotions or emotional concerns. The more powerful the underlying emotion, the more powerful (intense) is the Central Image of the dream.

Starting with the tidal wave dream in Chapter 2, we will discuss here many studies of dreams recorded in traumatic and other situations. This takes us directly into point 3 at the center of the Contemporary Theory. Then we will return to discuss the focused-waking-to-dreaming continuum (point 1 of the theory) and the remaining points.

My associates and I have conducted numerous investigations relating the central imagery of the dream to underlying emotion and especially showing that the intensity of the central imagery is related to the strength of the underlying emotion.

The tidal wave dream appears to be the clearest case. The tidal wave dream is always an intense and powerful image and appears to be related to the powerful emotion of the dreamer, especially in the cases we have studied after trauma. Here the person experiencing the tidal wave dream is clearly under the influence of emotions, which could be summarized as "I feel terrified" or "I feel overwhelmed." As we saw in Chapter 2, other emotions such as sadness, guilt, and anger are often pictured as well.

We first called the tidal wave image and similar powerful Central Images the "Contextualizing Image" (CI) since it appeared to provide a "picture-context" for the emotion of the dreamer (Hartmann 1996; Hartmann, Rosen, Gazells, and Moulton,1997; Hartmann, Rosen, and Grace 1998; Hartmann 1999). However, this term was considered unwieldy and confusing by some, so the image is now called simply the "Central Image," keeping the abbreviation CI. A scoring sheet for the CI has been developed (Figure 3.1) which can be used on any written or recorded dream report. It has now been used in about fifty different research studies.

The scorer, who knows nothing about the dreamer or the circumstances surrounding the dream, looks at a dream report and fills out the scoring sheet (Figure 3.1). She first decides whether or not there is a scorable Central Image. If there is (this turns out to be the case in 50% to 65% of dreams scored), the scorer jots down a few words describing the image and then scores the intensity of the image on a seven-point scale (0, 0.5, 1.0, 1.5, 2.0, 2.5, 3.0) based on how powerful, vivid, bizarre and detailed the image seems ("0" means no CI and "3" means about as powerful an image as you have seen in dreams). She then tries to guess what emotion or emotions, from a list of

Definition: A Central Image (contextualizing image) is a striking, arresting, or compelling image — not simply a story — but an image, which stands out by virtue of being especially powerful, vivid, bizarre, or detailed.

List of Emotions

1. fear, terror
2. helplessness, vulnerability, being trapped, being immobilized
3. anxiety, vigilance
4. despair, hopelessness (giving up)
5. anger, frustration
6. disturbing — cognitive dissonance, disorientation, weirdness
7. guilt
8. grief, loss, sadness, abandonment, disappointment
9. shame, inadequacy
10. disgust, repulsion
11. power, mastery supremacy
12. awe, wonder, mystery
13. happiness, joy, excitement
14. hope
15. peace, restfulness
16. longing
17. relief, safety
18. love (relationship)

Score the most intense image. Only if you can't decide – if there is a second image of about the same intensity – score the second image on a separate line.

Note: The Central Image can sometimes involve a short series of images. It can be a brief "central moving image." It does not have to be a static "snapshot."

Dream ID#	1. CI? (Y/N)	2. What is it?	3. Intensity (rate 0 – 3)	4. What emotion?	5. Second emotion?

Figure 3.1 Scoring dreams for the Central Image

emotions provided, might be pictured by this image. The Central Image Intensity (CII) turns out to be an especially important measure. Although it is of course a subjective judgment by the scorer, there is good agreement between scorers—inter-rater reliability of r = .70 to r = .90 (Hartmann 1998; Hartmann, Kunzendorf, Rosen, and Grace 2001a). We will discuss a number of studies using Central Image Intensity (CII) to examine the question of whether the power of the CI is related to the power of the underlying emotion.

Since there are eighteen emotions to choose from (Figure 3.1), it has been more difficult to obtain good inter-rater reliability on the individual emotion pictured by the dream imagery. However, there is quite good agreement between raters when emotions are grouped into three categories: 1) fear/terror and helplessness/vulnerability; 2) other negative emotions (#s 3-10 on the score sheet); and 3) all positive emotions (#s 11-18). (Hartmann, Zborowski, and Kunzendorf 2001b).

First we showed that, on a blind basis, CII is rated higher in dreams that in daydreams (Hartmann et al. 2001a), as expected. We also found, as expected, that CII is higher in content from REM awakenings than from non-REM awakenings, which in turn score higher than material from waking periods (Hartmann and Stickgold 2000). We then went on to look at whether CII is related to emotion and the power of the dreamer's emotion.

In one study we found that CII is rated higher in "dreams that stand out" than in "recent dreams" from the same persons (Hartmann et al. 2001a). Likewise, CII is scored higher in dreams characterized as "the earliest dream you can remember" than in "recent dreams" (Hartmann and Kunzendorf 2006-2007). Thus, CII appears to be high in dreams that are remembered and are presumably emotionally important.

We found that CII is especially high in dreams considered "big" dreams, no matter how these are defined. In one study we specifically examined dreams considered "important" by the dreamer. A group of 57 persons each sent us a recent dream they considered "important" and a dream they considered "unimportant" or less important. CII was significantly higher in the "important" dreams (mean for important dreams = 1.193; mean for unimportant dreams = 0.807; difference = 0.386; *S.D.* 1.048; $t = 2.78$; $p < .007$) (Hartmann, 2008a).

We also studied one group of "especially significant" dreams. A group of 23 students very interested in their dreams each reported one "especially significant" dream. The mean CII in these 23 dreams was 2.617 (means of two experienced raters). This is the highest mean CII score of any group we have seen, much higher than means of recent dreams in various groups. These students did not supply a "non-significant dream" for a direct comparison. However, comparing these "highly significant" dreams with our largest group of recent dreams, from 286 students, we found a highly significant difference: ($t = 16.0$; $p < .0001$) (Hartmann 2008a).

Similarly, we found very high CIIs in dreams considered "impactful" in the sense that they led the dreamer to produce a new work of science or art (Barrett 2001). The mean CII in this group of 34 dreams was 2.54 +/- 0.4, much higher than the mean value in our students.

We went on to examine dreams at times of trauma and stress—situations involving strong and mainly negative emotions. We were able to obtain long dream series from ten different persons who had recently experienced a variety of acute traumas. All of these dreams (451 dreams) were scored for CIs, on a blind basis, as above. In each of the ten trauma cases, the mean CI score was higher than the mean CI score of the student group (Hartmann, Zborowski, Rosen and Grace 2001c). Overall, the mean CI intensity for the dreams of the people experiencing trauma (a total of 451 dreams) was 1.43 +/- 0.49, compared to a student group (286 dreams from 286 students) which was 0.75 +/- 1.03; $t = 4.1$; $p <.001$ (see Figure 3.2). In four of the ten cases, a series of dreams before as well as immediately after trauma were available. In all four of these, the CI score was higher after trauma than before.

Since the student group differed greatly from the trauma group in sex distribution, age, and other ways, an age and gender matched subgroup of the students was formed. A subgroup of 30 students was formed, carefully matched with the trauma group for age and sex. Comparing the trauma group with these matched students again showed much higher scores in the

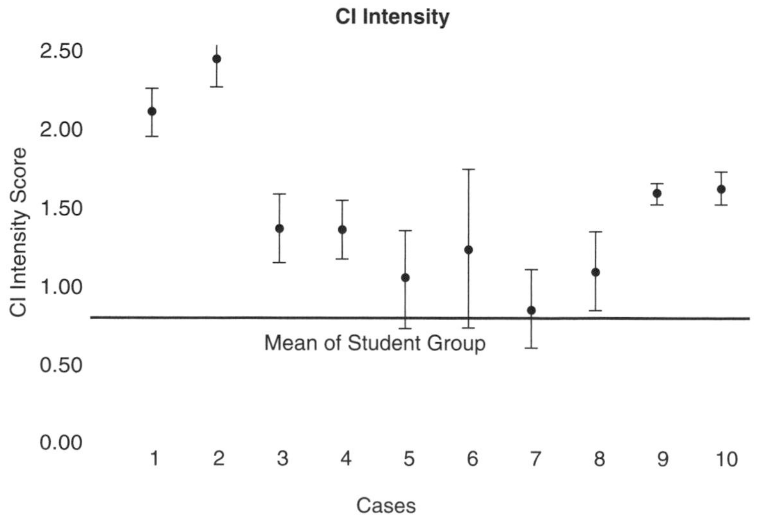

Figure 3.2 Central Image intensity after trauma

trauma group (1.43 =/- .49 vs. .57 +/- .92; $t = 3.6$; $p < .001$). CI scores in the trauma group were significantly higher than in this matched control group. (Hartmann et al. 1998; Hartmann et al. 2001c). The "emotion pictured" also showed a difference. The trauma group had more negative emotions, and especially more of emotions 1 and 2. The two cases with worst trauma (one violent rape, and one case of torture in a Central American country) had the highest CII scores, and also had "emotions pictured" scored as almost always emotions 1 (fear/terror) or 2 (helplessness/vulnerability).

In another study we looked at the effects of reported abuse. Three hundred and six students filled out several forms and questionnaires as part of a study on dreams and personality. One page was headed simply: "Please write down the most recent dream you can remember." Thus, 306 dream reports were available from this group. On another page, each student was asked to check off a number of items of demographic data. Here, subjects were asked to answer yes or no to the following six questions:

1. Have you experienced any physical abuse...in childhood? In adolescence? More recently?
2. Have you experienced any sexual abuse...in childhood? In adolescence? More recently?

(Thus, students were asked about two types of abuse at each of three time periods).

Relatively small numbers of students checked yes on any one of the six questions; however, we formed a sizeable group (N = 52) consisting of all students who answered yes to any one or more of the six questions.

All dreams were scored on a blind basis for CI intensity. Results showed that the 52 students reporting any abuse had a mean score of 1.12+/- 1.2, whereas the students reporting no abuse had a mean CI intensity of 0.65 +/- 1.0 (Figure 3.3). This is a significant difference (p = 2.63; p <.01). "Emotions pictured" in the "abuse" group showed higher levels of emotions 1 and 2 (fear/terror and helplessness/vulnerability).

We did not interview these students, so we have no way of knowing exactly what sorts of abuse they remembered. Nonetheless, the Central Image Intensity of a recent dream was sensitive to this report of abuse (Hartmann et al. 2001c).

THE 9/11 STUDY

The studies reviewed above are important but somewhat problematic. The types of trauma within each study differed; the number of dreams as well

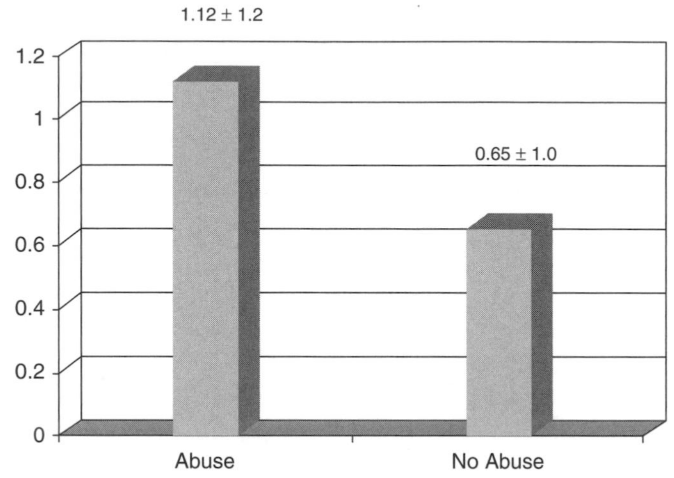

Figure 3.3 Central Image Intensity in students who report abuse or no abuse

$*t = 2.63$, $p = 0.01$

as the method of dream collection varied; and there was not always an opportunity to compare dreams before and after the trauma in the same individuals.

The terrorist attacks of 9/11/01 allow us to study these issues more systematically. There is considerable evidence that the events of 9/11 had widespread measurable effects on the psychological health of the U.S. population. Overall, even though most of the population did not experience trauma in the sense required for a diagnosis of PTSD, it appears likely that almost everyone in the U.S. was affected in some way. I believe it is fair to say that almost everyone probably experienced some mild form of trauma or at least emotional arousal, in the period following 9/11/01.

Since a sizable number of people have been recording all their remembered dreams for years, we had an opportunity to compare systematically recorded dreams before and after the events of 9/11. We were able to find 44 persons, living in various parts of the United States, who had recorded all of their dreams for many years and were willing to send us twenty dreams from their records: the last ten before 9/11/01 and the first ten after 9/11/01.

The 880 dreams obtained were then assigned random numbers and scored on a blind basis for the presence or absence of a CI and for CII. The dreams were also scored on what emotion might be pictured by the CI, and on two standard dream content scales: dream-likeness, and overall vividness. Length of the dream report was scored roughly as number of lines of text. Additionally, the dreams were scored on three ad-hoc scales for dream content: any content involving a) attacks of any kind; b) tall buildings or towers; and c) airplanes. Each of these three scales was scored from 0 (no such content) to 3 (very definite content of this kind).

The results of this study were surprisingly clear-cut (Table 3.1). The dreams after 9/11 did not contain more tall buildings, nor did they include more airplanes; however, the dreams after 9/11 did show a highly significant increase in Central Image Intensity, and in the proportion of dreams having CIs.

There was also an increase in dreams involving attacks, but this was a small change, much less significant, and with a smaller effect size, than the change in CI intensity. The attacks pictured involved mostly being chased by dangerous people, gangs, or monsters—in other words things very common in attack dreams or anxiety dreams in general.

In terms of the "emotions pictured" by the Central Images, there was a shift towards more fear/terror and helplessness/vulnerability. This finding did reach statistical significance but was not as great an effect as the intensity finding (Hartmann and Basile 2003; Hartmann and Brezler 2008).

These results are very consistent with what we have found in other studies. We find clear-cut significant results when we study Central Image Intensity. The higher CII scores are also related to more frequent scoring of emotions 1 and 2 being pictured ($p < .05$). The results on emotional scoring are less definite when we allow the rater to guess an emotion from the list of eighteen possible emotions, which makes exact agreement between raters difficult. Grouping the emotions does reveal an effect in the direction of more scores of emotions 1 and 2 from dreams after 9/11 in the studies mentioned.

All this research on trauma and on the effects of 9/11 shows that when we can know or estimate the power of the dreamer's emotion, the power of the Central Image of the dream appears to increase similarly. After trauma or stress, when the emotions felt can be presumed to be mainly fear and other negative emotions, the emotions fear/terror (1) and helplessness/vulnerability (2) are the ones rated as being pictured by the Central Image.

It is worth re-emphasizing that the increase in powerful images was the most significant finding in the 9/11 study, with the greatest effect size (eta-squared = 0.2). In fact, somewhat to our surprise, there were some very powerful dream images in the "after 9/11" group that were judged as picturing *positive emotions*. Here are two examples.

Table 3.1 Dreams Before and After 9-11-01

Measure	Mean (± SD)* before 9/11	Mean (± SD)* after 9/11	ANOVA: stats for after vs. before 9/11*			
			Deviation from grand mean	*F*	*p*	eta^2
CI Intensity	1.10 (± .43)	1.29 (± .41)	± .09	9.4	< .004**	.18
CI Proportion	0.71 (± .20)	0.79 (± .15)	± .04	11.6	< .001**	.22
Length(text-lines)	12.93 (± 9.79)*	11.88 (± 7.23)*	± .52	0.7	NS	
Dream-likeness	4.54 (± .92)	4.52 (± .93)	± .01	0.1	NS	
Vividness	3.85 (± .91)	3.94 (± .93)	± .04	0.7	NS	
Content: attacks	0.03 (± .09)	0.10 (± .14)	± .04	5.1	< .03**	.11
Content: towers	0.06 (± .09)	0.10 (± .16)	± .02	2.4	NS	
Content: airplanes	0.05 (± .10)	0.06 (± .11)	± .01	1.3	NS	

*Values are included only for the "within subjects" factor (after vs. before). The "between subjects" factor (gender) showed no significant effects. There were no significant interactions.

**Applying Bonferroni corrections as well as the less strict Sequential Bonferroni (Dunn-Sidak) corrections for multiple tests leads to the same conclusion: Results on "CI Intensity" and "CI Proportion" are still significant. Results on "Content: attacks" are no longer significant at $p < .05$. (Hartmann & Brezler 2008)

I am standing in my parents' kitchen on W. Avenue. I am starting to chant and I can feel a vibration coming up through my chest and heart area. There are tiny red flickering lights starting to form on the ceiling, followed by a new space that is starting to open. With my hands I feel the space and it feels different, heavier, or textured. Now I am outside and to my left is a man sitting in a chair watching me. Again I start to chant. The vibration coming from me sounds like a low rumble. To my right I see the same flickering red lights and then a white glow appears, but not hot, not fire. I see what I would imagine a vortex to be. I wake up from this dream chanting!

I am walking with Jim on a downtown city street near some warehouses. Our dog decides to take a poop in the middle of the street and stops traffic. A truck is nearby and an owl appears in the passenger-side window. I am surprised and delighted and point this out to Jim. The owl is large with a white face and a reddish brown body. Now a second one appears—larger than the first— and now a third in the window of the building right next to us. She is huge, maybe six feet tall, and I feel suddenly like I must be quiet and start walking away quietly.

Both of these dreams were rated very high on Central Image Intensity, and in both the emotion pictured was judged to be "awe, wonder, mystery."

Another intriguing finding emerged from this study. Although all of the participants had seen the events of 9/11 on television numerous times, not a single dream actually pictured planes hitting tall towers or anything close to that. It seems that a dream always makes new connections. The dream is a creation, not simply a replay. This will be discussed in more detail in Chapter 4.

If indeed a dream involves picturing of an emotion and if the intensity of the image somehow measures the strength of the emotion, we might try to start with the emotion and see whether we could produce a dream. In other words, can we create a dream "in the laboratory" using this model? We have done one research study in which a group of students was asked to write down a recent dream, a recent daydream, a daydream experienced in class under instructions to simply allow imagery to develop, and finally a daydream experienced in class after the students had been asked to choose an emotion close to them and to feel it very intensely. All the descriptions were scored on a blind basis. The last condition, which could be called "imagery under the influence of strong emotion," produced results that were scored just as bizarre and as "dream-like" as recent dreams (Hartmann et al. 2002-2003). For instance, here are two examples of the imagery produced under emotion, one by a male and one by a female student:

> *I saw a mountaintop with a sun rising. A man was standing on top of the mountain. He was looking around and it was very peaceful. He began to stretch and he turned into a dragon. The dragon then flew away.*
>
> *I was standing in a circle, surrounded by people I knew. The circle kept getting closer to me. Then I became enclosed by a circle of flames, and I was slowly sucked into this black hole type of thing.*

Here it certainly appears that something very like a dream was indeed produced in these students who were of course awake at the time. Perhaps imagery under the influence of strong emotion can produce a dream or something fairly dream-like without the presence of sleep.

On a number of occasions I have also asked participants in a workshop to do the same thing—to concentrate on an emotion that was already present, then to intensify it as much as they could, and then allow imagery to develop.

Here are a few examples of the imagery that emerged, along with the emotion they had intensified, that led to the images:

> *I had wings, big wings, almost like an angel. I flew around the sky and saw the whole world from up high. (Emotion: joy)*
>
> *I'm on a black-green mossy rock. I'm looking up at this other woman who's all pink and glowing. (Emotion: longing, envy)*
>
> *I see a deer caught in a car's headlights. It's frozen, totally helpless. (Emotion: fear)*
>
> *I have a real ugly pustule. A big bug comes crawling out of it and becomes a lobster. (Emotion: anger and disgust)*
>
> *I was on some kind of rough ground that was moving under me. I kept fighting to stay up, stay standing, but I kept falling down, over and over. (Emotion: frustration)*

I usually ask the participants a few questions about this imagery, such as "was it like a dream?" Very often the answer is "yes, it was like a fragment of a dream or a vivid piece of a dream."

I cannot say that we definitely created dreams in the workshop. However, we demonstrated that even without sleep, in a relaxed waking state, when we allow imagery to develop in the presence of a powerful emotion, something can emerge which is much like the Central Image (CI) of a dream. I believe this lends support to the idea that dreams involve imagery under the influence of emotion.

Of course a dream seldom consists solely of a Central Image, although this does happen and as mentioned the CI is the part of the dream that stays in the memory or is easily recalled and much of the dream is forgotten. But what of the rest of the dream? Usually the CI occurs in, and is part of, a story or context. We are always making up stories and placing things in context, but this is not unique to dreaming (see Chapter 7).

4 A Dream Is a Creation, Not a Replay. A Dream Always Makes New Connections, Guided by Emotion

Dreaming always makes new connections. It does not replay what was experienced in waking life. Even dreams usually thought of as replays—for instance repetitive or recurrent dreams, and traumatic (PTSD) dreams, turn out to be new creations, not replays. As a new creation, guided by emotion, the dream is somewhat like a work of art. Painting and film are sometimes derived directly from dreams, so it is easy to see similarities between these art forms and dreaming. I will argue for similarities between dreaming and other forms of art as well. I examine poetry and dreams, suggesting that the "objective correlative" of a poem is very like the Central Image of a dream.

One important point which emerges from the many studies reviewed above is that dreaming involves making connections, and often these are new connections, not yet made by the waking mind. Dreaming is not a replay of what was experienced in waking.

There is a view that dreaming, or at least dreaming in REM sleep, involves a repetition or replay of material experienced in waking and thus dreaming is involved in the consolidation of memory. This view is based on the frequent appearance of bits of waking experiences in dreams ("day residue") and on recent studies showing that hippocampal "place cells" in rats fire during REM in a pattern similar to their firing while the rats navigated a maze some hours earlier (Qin, McNaughton, Skaggs, and Barnes 1997; Wilson and McNaughton 1994). Studies of human dream content do not support the idea of a "replay" as we shall see. I do believe that dreaming plays a role in memory formation, but the role is not consolidation of memory. Rather dreaming "weaves in" and integrates new material into existing memory, guided by emotion (see Chapter 11).

A dream may certainly incorporate events that occur the day or days before the dream (the "day residue"). However, the dream does not simply repeat the material, but changes it and weaves it into an ongoing story. Thinking of typical dream settings, for instance, a dream may indeed take place in a specific spot or town known to you, but just as often the setting is a combination of several places. (I often dream of a city that's Boston, but it's also New York. Both are cities that I have lived in and know well. Even if the setting is definitely one city, the more details I remember, the more it seems that it's not exactly the same as the city I know in waking life.) Or the setting may be generic—a big city, or an open plain—but when you think about it carefully it reminds you of several places you know. And the characters may be people you know, or strangers, or people who seem familiar but you're not sure who they are. And the characters are notoriously shifty—they are sometimes two people at once, or one person, but he's not quite right, there's something different about him, he looks a bit like someone else.

In terms of actions or occurrences in the dream, a dream does sometimes refer to or "picks up" something that happened recently, most often on the day of the dream. This is known as *day residue,* discussed in detail by Freud and many others. However, the dream does not replay exactly what happened, but it takes a piece of it and combines it with other material. There's never (I should say "almost never" to be on the safe side) a longish replay of something actually seen or experienced during waking, even if it's a powerful or emotional event.

In the many series of dreams after trauma reviewed in the last chapter—and see also Chapter 11—I have never seen a dream that replayed the traumatic events or other events exactly as they occurred. And, as I mentioned, in our study of dreams before and after 9/11/01, not a single one of the 880 dreams (440 of them after 9/11) involved planes hitting tall buildings or similar scenarios, even though all the participants had seen this many times on television (and it was clearly an emotionally important experience). No scenes were pictured that were even close to the actual attacks. So even something as striking as the 9/11 attacks does not generally make it into dreams as a replay.

I should mention that I do have two reports of dreams that more or less pictured the 9/11 attacks, though neither of them occurred within our research study, and it may be instructive to exam these. The two dreams were reported three months, and eight months, respectively, after 9/11/01, by two middle-aged men, each of whom was undergoing severe personal stress at the time of the dream—in one case the breakup of an important long-term relationship, and in the other case a myocardial infarction (heart attack) followed by immediate quadruple bypass coronary surgery. Both men were interested in their dreams, and had expressed surprise that they had had no dreams of the terrorist attacks—until these intensely stressful personal events occurred. Even in these two dreams, the "replay" was not actually a replay of the scene they had repeatedly seen on TV. In the more clearly remembered dream, the dreamer himself was inside a tall building similar to the World Trade Center buildings when there was an explosion higher up, and glass started falling all around. (Actually this dreamer lived several hundred miles from New York City and had been in the towers himself only once, ten years previously).

If we can generalize from our sample, it appears that the terrorist attack scenario is not dreamt about simply as a result of having been seen repeatedly. Rather, the 9/11 images of planes hitting towers have become "tidal waves!" This imagery, or rather the ability to reconstruct similar or related imagery, seems to be stored in a manner similar to the tidal wave, which we can summon in our dreams at times of personal emotional stress. The results also support the view that these powerful dream images are new creations, guided by strong emotion, not replays of waking experiences and it is worth noting that even in these two cases, where the 9/11 events did occur, they occurred in an altered form. They were not simple replays of what had been seen on TV.

But aren't there exceptions—for instance, aren't there many reports of "recurrent dreams"? Recurrent dreams have indeed been the subject of a number of studies (Cartwright and Romanek 1978; Domhoff 1996; Robbins and Houshi 1983). Usually they are frightening dreams often beginning in childhood. However, these dreams are really dreams about a recurrent theme. In my experience they are never, or almost never, precisely repetitive dreams. The general theme may be the same, but there are usually changes in the dream as the dreamer's life, and the dreamer's emotional state, changes.

A patient in psychoanalysis provided an especially clear series of nightmares, which appeared to reflect her mental state. This very intelligent young woman did report having recurrent dreams. She described a series of dreams going back many years, which involved sharks or shark-like monsters chasing her in the ocean. In one dream she was held captive by shark-monsters who were going to torture or kill her. The details varied, but the dangerous shark theme was constant. These dreams seemed to occur especially when some important change was happening in her life. They also occurred a number of times during her psychoanalysis, at the times when she was unsure of herself and when she seemed to be re-experiencing childhood fears and childhood helplessness. Over the course of several years she made gradual progress in understanding her life and overcoming her fears. During this time she had several more dreams of sharks, but the sharks gradually became less terrifying than before. She no longer woke up scared whenever she dreamt of a shark. Finally, at a time when she was finishing her treatment, when her life and work were going well, she had one final dream of a shark. This time she was at a swimming pool rather than in the ocean. A friendly little shark came out of the swimming pool right next to her. She patted it on the head and it curled up at her feet like a pet dog (Hartmann 1984)! Obviously the "recurrent dreams" here kept the theme of a shark, but changed to reflect her emotional state. They were not exactly repetitive, and obviously, they were not replays of actual events.

Does this mean that there is no such thing as a truly repetitive dream? No, such repetitive dreams do exist, where the same dreams are repeated over and over again. There is in fact one situation in which the same dream is indeed experienced again and again—the post-traumatic dreams that occur in PTSD (post traumatic stress disorder). I have studied such dreams both in my research work and in clinical work with veterans. However, even these repetitive dreams on examination turn out to be creations, not simple replays of waking events.

Often the veteran suffering from PTSD says, "The dream is just the way it was… I was in a foxhole…noise all around me… a shell came flying… just the way it was!" But in all the cases I have examined in detail, the dream is not "just the way it was." There's at least one important change. For instance, one of the most common dreams in Vietnam veterans goes something like this, "I'm back there in the foxhole. Just the way it was. There's noise all around. A shell explodes right in front of me. I scream and I'm dying as I wake up." What actually happened was a shell exploded and killed the man's buddy—his best friend—who was in the foxhole with him, or somewhere nearby. The dream does not simply replay the event. It adds a slight change: the dreamer himself is dying rather than his buddy. This appears to be a replay of the events, but slightly altered, probably by an emotion—the emotion known as survivor guilt: the dreamer feels guilty that he survived while his buddy died. Thus, even these so-called repetitive post-traumatic dreams involve the making of new connections. These dreams too turn out to be creations, not simple replays of events.

The most dramatic example in my experience occurred in a Vietnam veteran who suffered for years from PTSD. He had been a medical corpsman and his job consisted of working just behind the front lines, loading wounded soldiers and body bags off of a helicopter returning from the lines. His job involved getting the wounded men to the right places for treatment and properly identifying dead soldiers in the body bags. The most traumatic event he experienced occurred just after a serious battle. He was opening body bags one after another and found his best buddy in the last body bag he opened. He has dreamt about his experience over and over again for many years. He indeed does have a repetitive dream, which occurs unaltered time after time. In describing the dream he says, "I open up the body bags one by one, I zip open the last body bag. The body inside is ME, and I wake up screaming." Obviously he has taken a serious traumatic incident and changed it slightly in his dreams so that it is he rather than his friend who has died. One can see this dream as picturing terror and vulnerability, but also guilt, related to his having survived while his buddy died. So even here, in a repetitive PTSD dream, something new has been added. The repetitive dream is not simply a replay of waking events. My colleagues and I have found a great many traumatic dreams with a very similar structure.

Returning to dreams in general, my conclusion is that new connections are always involved and sometimes these connections can be very useful to us. For instance, they can help us see new facts or possibilities in our lives, as we will discuss in Chapter 6. These new connections can also produce new works of art and science (numerous examples are cited in Barrett 1992). Of course, this only happens when the mind is prepared, and I would add that the problem must be an emotional concern of the dreamer. Elias Howe, who had a dream that led to the design of the sewing machine, had been trying for a long time to invent a workable model, so the problem was immensely important to him. In this sense dreams can sometimes solve problems (see Chapter 11).

THE DREAM AND THE WORK OF ART

A dream makes new connections and can itself be considered a creative product. In this sense, a dream is similar to a work of art. Creating a work of art has been defined in many ways, usually emphasizing that old materials are put together in a new way. I have summarized this and added that this "putting together" is obviously influenced by the artist's emotion (Hartmann 1999). This is not a random process, of course: materials are put together in a way that expresses an underlying emotion or emotional theme. In other words, art in general can be thought of as making new connections guided by emotions, which is just what we have been saying about dreaming.

Film and painting are sometimes consciously based on dreams, and films are often considered the most oneiric (dreamlike) of the arts. But other arts are based on dreams as well. A number of writers have attributed their poems or stories to dreams. Robert Louis Stevenson famously stated that his stories came to him directly from his dreams invented by his "committee of sleep" (Stevenson 1892). Some understand this to mean that the stories actually came to him word for word in his dreams. From my experience I consider this unlikely. I would suggest that a powerful image came to him in a dream—for instance, a well-dressed physician turning into a monster (not an uncommon type of nightmare image) and he then proceeded to fill in the details and write *Dr. Jekyll and Mr. Hyde* using his well-developed novelistic skills.

I believe that poems too often have a powerful Central Image. In fact, what T.S. Eliot has called the "objective correlative" of a poem is strikingly similar to what we have called the Central Image of a dream. For instance, consider the image that Eliot himself cites, when discussing the objective correlative, from his poem "The Love Song of J. Alfred Prufrock" (Eliot 1917):

"I should have been a pair of ragged claws
Scuttling across the floors of silent seas."

This powerful image, occurring starkly in the middle of the poem, pictures the social shyness of the narrator who feels uncomfortable with the women who "come and go speaking of Michelangelo." Here the image obviously pictures an emotional concern. At the beginning of the same poem there is a startling image picturing an emotional tone that is more difficult to specify in one word.

"Let us go then you and I
when the evening is spread out against the sky
like a patient etherized upon a table."

This image does set an emotional mood for the dream and perhaps pictures an emotional state. This state suggests a state of disturbance, uneasiness, or dissonance.

The work of art—the painting or poem, if it is successful—can be thought of as providing an emotional bridge between the artist and the viewer or audience. The emotion or emotional concerns of the artist guide or produce the work, which pictures the emotion. The work or image then in turn produces the same or a similar emotion in the audience seeing or hearing the work.

Likewise the dream, or especially the CI of the dream, when it is told or read, can be thought of as providing an emotional bridge (Figure 4.1). The emotion pulls together connections in the dreamer and produces the dream. But then the dream, especially the CI of the dream, when it is heard or read, produces the same or similar emotion in the listener, or therapist, or the scorer who is judging what emotion might be pictured.

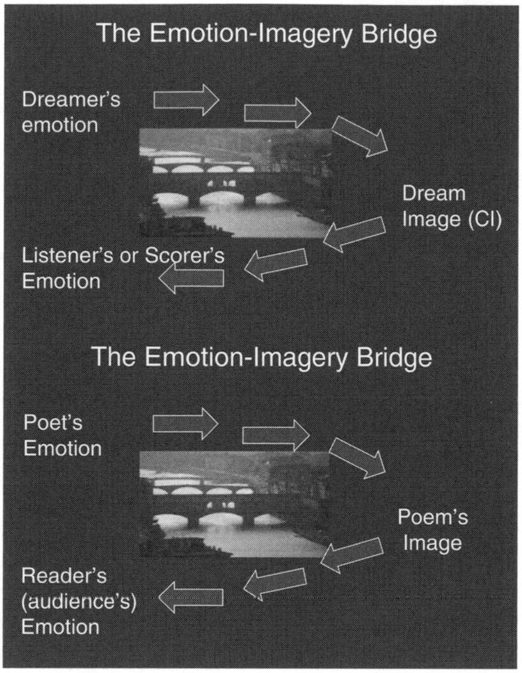

Figure 4.1 The Emotion-Imagery Bridge

The reader may feel that I have gone a bit overboard here, and in a sense I have. I am certainly not suggesting that most dreams are fully formed works of art. Obviously there are differences and most dreams can at best be called bits and pieces of a work or a rough attempt, rather than a true work of art. However, my main point is to emphasize not an identity but a similarity in the basic mechanism of dreaming and the basic mechanism of creating art: old material is connected and put together in new ways, guided by emotion. In the next chapter we will see that dreaming and artistic creation both happen most readily when we are at one end of our continuum of mental functioning.

5 The Focused-Waking-Thought–to–Dreaming Continuum. Dreaming Is One End of a Continuum

Dreaming is a form of mental functioning. It is not an alien intrusion. It is one end of a continuum of mental functioning (which means chiefly cerebral cortical functioning) running from focused waking thought at one end, through fantasy and daydreaming, to dreaming at the other. Though we intuitively think of dreaming as "totally different" from the other forms of mental functioning, careful examination reveals a great deal of overlap between fantasy/daydreaming and dreaming.

At first glance dreams appear so different and alien—not a part of us—that they have often been considered messages from the gods, or coded messages from some sacred place. Even those who believe dreams are created by our minds nonetheless consider dreams to be in a strange foreign language, different from the language of our normal waking minds (Freud and others). I will try to demonstrate here that dreaming is simply one form of mental functioning—part of a continuum. It is not an alien intrusion. It is not a distinct and isolated activity that bears little connection to other forms of mental activity. On a biological level, mental functioning refers to the functioning of the brain and especially the functioning of the cerebral cortex. The biology of dreaming will be discussed further in Chapter 8.

The continuum I propose, which we have studied in detail, runs roughly from focused-waking-thought at one end through looser thought or reverie to fantasy, daydreaming, and eventually to dreaming. This sort of continuum can be pictured in a number of different ways (Figures 5.1 and 5.2).

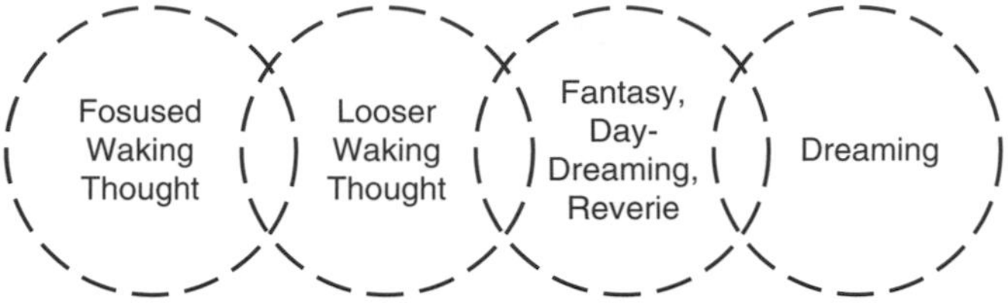

Figure 5.1 A Continuum of Mental Functioning

Of course, the four overlapping circles in Figure 5.1 are an oversimplification. Many other mental states or forms of functioning are not listed—for instance hypnagogic imagery, drug-induced states, hallucinations, etc, but these can readily be fit into the continuum. I need to discuss the continuum in detail because for most of us the idea is not intuitively obvious. Our tendency is to think of our dreams as somehow "totally different" even though we may admit that the dreams must be produced somewhere in our minds and brains.

	Focused Waking thought	Looser, Less-structured Waking thought	Reverie free association daydreaming	Dreaming
What dealt with?	Percepts: Math symbols Signs, words	fewer words, signs, more visual-spatial imagery		almost pure imagery
How?	logical relationship If A then B	less logic, more noting or picturing of similarities, More metaphor		almost pure picture - metaphor in "typical dreams"
Self-reflection:	highly self-reflective — "I know I am sitting here reading."	less self-reflective more "caught up" in the process, the imagery		total thereness, no self-reflection
Boundaries:	solid divisions, Categorizations, thick boundaries	less rigid categorization, thinner boundaries		merging condensation loosening of categories, thin boundaries
Sequencing; Connections	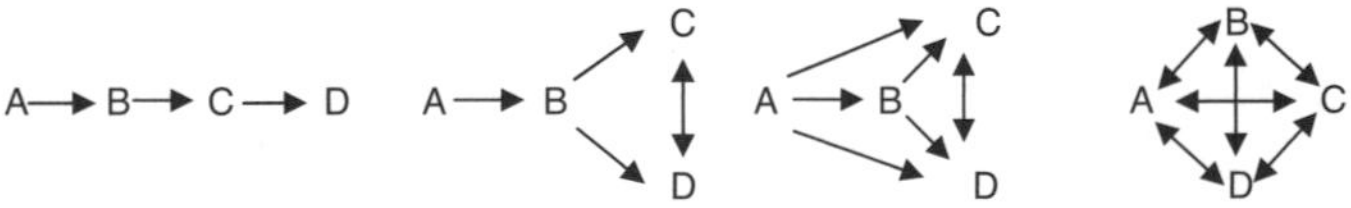			
Processing:	relatively serial; net functions chiefly as a feed-forward net			net functions more as an auto-associative net;
Subsystems:	activity chiefly within structures subsystem			activity less within, more across or outside of, Structured subsystems

Figure 5.2 A continuum of mental functioning: details

In fact, dreams do appear in some ways to be so different from our normal waking thoughts and fantasy that for a long time, in various cultures, dreams were considered to be obviously coming from somewhere else: from the gods, or from God, or from the devil. For most of us, even though we may not subscribe to these views, the dream seems "totally different" from the remainder of our mental lives in a number of major ways. It is worth discussing these apparently major differences, which turn out not to be as absolute as they seem.

These include the view that the dream is perceptual, not conceptual—in other words we picture rather than think; the view that dreams are "bizarre"; that dreaming is "so real"; that dreaming is so fleeting, so easily forgotten; that dreaming is involuntary—we have no control; and finally that dreaming must be totally different because we're asleep when it happens, or because we're in the unique state of REM-sleep. I'll discuss these in turn, and show that for each of these differences, there is actually considerable overlap, not a clear separation. And we'll also look at some studies presenting positive evidence of overlap or similarity between the forms of mental functioning. However, I want to make it clear that I am by no means saying that dreaming is like thinking. Not at all! They're at opposite ends of the continuum. But I'll demonstrate that there is a lot of overlap between adjacent types of mental functioning.

First of all, for most of us, there seems to be little formal thought in dreams. Our dreams seem to be pure imagery rather than thought. We appear to cogitate, plan, and plot very little in our dreams. The dreams seem to be made up almost entirely of imagery—especially, for most of us—visual imagery. This has been summarized in the view that dreams are perceptual rather than conceptual.

It is certainly true that in dreams we are far from our focused waking thought mode, but there is no sudden break or discontinuity between fantasies/daydreams and dreams. Consider our typical daydreams. For most of us, daydreams are perceptual, especially visual. They involve much more picturing and feeling than thinking. We may have a daydream about a wonderful vacation on the beach, eating a perfect banquet, having sex with a movie star, etc. We picture something we'd like, or at times a scenario we don't like—a boss getting mad and firing us or a man threatening us with a gun. These are usually pictures and they are obviously guided by emotion. They are more like dreams on this dimension than what we are doing when we work on a mathematical problem. And in fact we have data showing that daydreams at times cannot be distinguished from dreams (Kunzendorf, Hartmann, Cohen, and Cutler 1997). Furthermore, although thought is not usually prominent, it is not absent in dreams either, as shown in a number of studies (Kozmova and Wolfman 2006; Purcell, Mullington,

Moffitt, Hoffman, and Pigeau 1986). It's a matter of degree, rather than all or nothing.

Dreams are sometimes considered totally different because they are so "bizarre." Strange things happen in dreams that never happen to us in reality: we sometimes fly; we occasionally see strange impossible creatures. Indeed, bizarreness does occur in dreams and there are scales to measure it (Winget and Kramer 1979). But several points are worth noting. First of all, the great majority of dreams turn out to be very ordinary—the bizarreness ratings are very low (Domhoff 2007; Dorus, Dorus, and Rechtschaffen 1971; Snyder 1970). We only occasionally have a truly bizarre or weird dream, though it is true that for some of us such a dream may be so striking that it remains in our memories for a long time. As we have discussed, the powerful Central Image, whether bizarre or not, is what makes a dream memorable, makes it stay on our minds.

Conversely, bizarreness is by no means restricted to dreams. Some people have daydreams or fantasies that are surprisingly bizarre. In one study, we found that when dreams and daydreams were scored on a blind basis, dreams overall were indeed scored as more "bizarre" and more "dream-like" (using well-established scales) than daydreams. However, the daydreams of one group of students—those characterized by thin boundaries (see Chapter 10)—were scored as being just as bizarre and just as dream-like as the night dreams of another group of students—those with thicker boundaries. Here is one example from our study (Kunzendorf et al. 1997).

> *I am seeing outlines of things. Then I see what appears to be an eye. The eye blinks and the surroundings jumble around and turn to mist. There seems to be a pit with levels of ledges. That is the only way to go but I don't go down there. I stay my ground and wait and wait but nothing happens till I look up and try to reach a light and then turn around and get comforted by the warm darkness that surrounds this place.*

This was a daydream reported by one of the students with "thin boundaries." So although bizarreness does sometimes occur in dreams, it is not restricted to dreams. If we try to catch what's going through our minds as we shave or brush our teeth, we find pretty bizarre material. Also, Foulkes and Vogel (1965) found that quite bizarre material occurs as we are falling asleep. Bizarreness is not restricted to dreams but appears increasingly as we examine material along the continuum towards fantasy, daydreaming, and dreaming.

In the next chapter, we will examine the way dreams are hyper-connective, compared to waking thought. Material is brought together more broadly and loosely, and this sometimes produces an image so unlike our ordinary waking experience that we call it bizarre.

Another way dreams are considered "totally different" is that they often seem to have a powerful feeling of reality—a feeling that we are "right there"—which our thoughts and daydreams lack. I agree that this is definitely a sensation found in most (though not all) dreams. We are totally involved in whatever scene we are experiencing and we are not aware that we are in bed sleeping. This occurs especially in dreams from REM sleep and is probably related to the biology of REM sleep, especially the low levels of norepinephrine, which will be discussed later (in Chapter 8). But even this sense of reality is not entirely unique to dreams. In one study, people described daydreams to me that were just as "real" as their night dreams. A number of the participants, who had many nightmares at night, also described having "daymares"—daydreams that became totally real and very frightening.

Here is another example of a daydream from the study just mentioned.

> *Me and two of my friends were going to a Halloween party. We were almost there when we looked back and noticed that someone had been following us. It was a tall, dark, hairy, rounded figure with wings. It ate us!*

Likewise hypnagogic imagery as we are falling asleep often feels totally real. And of course there are special states that feel totally real, such as hallucinations related to drugs, unusual medical conditions, or mental illness.

For some of us, our poor recall of our dreams appears very striking, apparently differentiating it from waking cognition. It is very common for us to have a vivid dream and then to totally forget it a few minutes after waking, unless we write it down or take some other step to make sure we remember. And again there is a brain biology that underlies the difficulty in remembering (see Chapter 11). But again, this ease of forgetting does not really distinguish dreams from a lot of our other mental activity. There is no question that our memory is good when we are dealing with a focused-waking activity, which we have labeled as important — a meeting with a significant person, an important plan, solving a problem, etc. But what of our memory of bits of daydreams and fantasies? Do we remember much of the images that were going through our minds while brushing our teeth this morning? Or fleeting daydreams while lying in bed awake last night? The data suggest that memory for such waking imagery, which has not been labeled as important, is just as poor as it is for dreams. (Klinger 1990; Singer 1993)

Then there is the lack of voluntary control in dreams. Things just seem to happen, completely out of our control. We appear to have no free will in dreams, as I discussed in detail in a paper long ago (Hartmann 1966). But again this lack of control is not entirely unique to dreams and it is not always found in dreams. As we noted above, many people with frequent nightmares also reported frightening daydreams and several of them spontaneously called these experiences "daymares." They would say something like, "I was having a nice daydream, but then it gradually became scarier and it ran away with me. I couldn't stop it" (Hartmann 1984). These daymares obviously have the scary and out-of-control characteristics of the dreams we know as nightmares.

Furthermore, control is not totally lacking in dreams. A great many people—over 25 percent by some estimates—experience lucid dreams—dreams in which they know they are dreaming. Sometimes people wake up quickly after such realization, but some are able to continue dreaming. Good lucid dreamers are often proud of their ability to remain in a dream and to control the dream to a great extent without waking up. Thus if they are having a nightmare, they will realize they are dreaming and then be able to run away from the monster if a monster is chasing them, or simply destroy the monster, or tame the monster and have a dialogue with it. They tell themselves that since they are dreaming they can fly and then proceed to fly off to visit far-off places or people, or visit dead relatives and have conversations with them (Gackenbach 1991; LaBerge 1985). In theses situations, even though the dream is continuing—and REM sleep is continuing (LaBerge, Levitan, and Dement 1986)—the lack of control is no longer present. The person is able to control the activity and does have a certain measure of free will. This control in dreams varies a great deal and there is a whole paper called "How lucid are lucid dreams" (Barrett 1992) which makes it clear that there is a wide range of ability to control the dream. Overall, I'd agree that lack of control in dreams is usually present, but it is certainly not invariable, nor is lack of control restricted to dreams.

It is also relevant to our discussion of the continuum to note that a lucid dream—especially one in which the dreamer is in control—may begin to resemble a daydream, in which one is usually more in control. I have spoken with some frequent lucid dreamers who dislike this analogy, claiming that their lucid dreams feel very different, subjectively, from their daydreams. However, my impression is that these were people whose daydreams were not very vivid or powerful. Others disagree with them. I have spoken to one very well known lucid dreamer, Peter Worsley in England, who has written about his many years of experiencing lucid dreaming (1988). He apparently experiences vivid daydreams too and he told me that he sometimes lies in bed awake and purposely goes into a vivid daydream, which then sometimes seems to become a lucid dream. For him the distance between lucid dreams and vivid daydreams is small, and the distinction not always clear.

Finally, the fact that dreams awaken us from sleep makes some people certain that dreams are "totally different" from other forms of mental functioning. After all, Aristotle's original definition of dreaming was simply "mental activity during sleep." Usually they are talking about the contrast between the world of a vivid dream and the world they awaken into. It's a whole different setting, different characters, etc. But again I have to point out that this sense is extremely clear only when we've had a dream that's very vivid, perceptual, "real." It's much less clear when we awaken from a more thought-like or fantasy-like dream, or a dreamlike state in which we're not sure we were really dreaming. And again, those who have very vivid, "real" daydreams, such as those with "daymares," describe a sense of coming out of it or jerking themselves back into reality that sounds not so different from waking up from a dream.

In recent years, based on biological research on REM and non-REM sleep (NREM), some have considered dreaming "totally different" since dreaming occurs in a separate biological state (REM sleep). This is not persuasive. Most dreaming does indeed arise from REM sleep, but this does not make a solid case that the dream itself need be totally different. I have spent years studying REM sleep and I certainly agree that it is a separate organismic state, with clear biological differences throughout the body from NREM sleep and from waking (Hartmann 1965; Jouvet 1962a; Snyder 1965). REM sleep activation at the cortex typically produces the cortical activity patterns that underlie what we call dreaming. However, it is gradually becoming clear that the same or similar patterns of cortical activity can occur at times without REM sleep. Some very dreamlike and bizarre material sometimes arises from awakenings at sleep onset (Foulkes and Vogel 1965) or in NREM sleep (Foulkes 1966; Suzuki et al. 2004), and conversely, some REM awakenings result in quite thought-like reports (Foulkes 1966).

Also, work by Solms (1997) and by Yu (2006) demonstrates that in patients who have experienced various types of brain damage, those with damage to certain cortical areas (see Chapter 11) say that they have completely stopped dreaming since their stroke or other brain event. Yet they continue to have REM sleep as before. It is the cortical activity pattern, not the fact of REM sleep that underlies dreaming. So I believe that the usual occurrence of dreams in REM sleep cannot convince us that the dream itself is totally separable from other forms of mental activity.

For all of these reasons, I believe it is useful to consider dreaming as part of a continuum. Certainly, dreams are different from waking thought in many ways, but they are not totally different from daydreams or fantasy, which in turn are not so different from reverie or ordinary loose waking thought. This should not prevent us, and it does not prevent me, from being awed and impressed by an occasional amazing dream. In fact, we do sometimes have striking images, important insights and occasionally new discoveries in dreams. Of course this also sometimes occurs in daydreams.

I have reviewed above a number of reasons that we sometimes consider dreams "totally different" and for each reason we have noticed that there is actually considerable overlap between the parts of the continuum. There is, furthermore, a great deal of positive evidence supporting the idea of similarity across the continuum or at least considerable overlap. For instance, our study on scoring of dreams and daydreams (mentioned above) demonstrates that daydreams often are surprisingly similar to dreams and cannot be distinguished from dreams by blind scorers (Kunzendorf et al. 1997). Domhoff and his collaborators (reviewed in Domhoff 1996, 2003) provide evidence that dreaming is in many ways continuous with waking fantasy and daydreams. They find, in long dream series, that a person's dreaming concerns are very similar to the same person's waking concerns. They also find that there is more continuity between dreaming and waking fantasy than between dreaming and waking behavior (Domhoff 2007). Similarly, Schredl has shown in several studies that a person's dreaming concerns are very similar to the same person's waking concerns (2007).

My collaborators and I demonstrated that under the influence of emotion, daydreams can become extremely dreamlike (Kunzendorf, Hartmann, Thomas, and Berensen 1999-2000). A group of students was asked to write down a recent dream, a recent daydream, a daydream that developed over five minutes (sitting in class, awake), and a daydream that developed (in class) while they experienced a strong emotion. Judges scored the material under the last condition (daydreams under emotion) to be just as dreamlike as the students' recent dreams.

These same conclusions about overlap come from studies that start with daydreams rather than dreams. Eric Klinger, who spent much of his professional life studying daydreams and fantasy, has written an entire book on daydreaming. One of his conclusions, after reviewing many detailed studies of daydreams, is very similar to what I have suggested above.

> *The style in which we daydream, which reflects our individuality as daydreamers, extends to the style in which we dream at night. True, dreams are on average looser, wilder, and more vivid. And during most dreams—excepting only the occasional "lucid" dream when we know we are dreaming—we become totally immersed, and the dream feels like reality. Yet daydreams sometimes take on some of that feeling of reality as well. This makes the conclusion that dreams are on a continuum with night dreams, rather than sharply different phenomena, hard to dodge* (Klinger 1990, p. 64).

Kozmová and Wolman (2006) and Purcell, Mullington, Moffitt, Hoffmann, and Pigeau (1986) have studied thought processes in dreams and have found that thinking is by no means absent in dreaming. It may be less prominent and sometimes overwhelmed by action and feeling, but it can still be detected and studied.

Singer (1988, 1993) studied ongoing conscious activity in normal individuals engaged in dull monitoring tasks. He summarizes his results: "I have found that samples of ongoing conscious thought of normal individuals include many of the metaphors or symbols that are also reported by them in recounting subsequent night dreams, i.e., the ongoing consciousness is already laying the groundwork for what seem to be the strange or creative settings of the night dream" (Singer 1993, 107).

Reinsel, Antrobus, and Wollman (1992) conducted a detailed study of persons under conditions of sensory isolation. In this situation, the subjects' waking fantasies were scored just as bizarre as their dreams.

Suzuki and colleagues (2004) provide good evidence that quite dream-like dreams can occur at times in NREM sleep—even in the first NREM period at the beginning of the night, when the dream cannot be considered to be recall of a previous REM dream.

Foulkes and his collaborators have shown that the ability to dream develops in childhood at age 4–10 concomitantly with the ability for waking visuo-spatial thinking (Foulkes 1982; Foulkes 1999; Foulkes, Hollifield, Bradley, Terry, and Sullivan 1991). Strikingly, the children who have better developed visuo-spatial abilities also have better developed dreaming. Daydreaming involves the same or similar visuo-spatial abilities and Foulkes believes that the development of daydreaming shows the same pattern as the development of dreaming, though he has not studied daydreaming as thoroughly (Foulkes 2009, personal communication). Again, this suggests that dreaming is part of a continuum of mental functioning.

Finally, there is evidence from studies of brain lesions showing that roughly the same regions and pathways are involved in visual dreaming and in visual waking processes such as fantasy and daydreaming. Mark Solms, reviewing the world's literature on the rare cases in which a brain lesion resulted in cessation of visual dreaming, says: "The most robust finding was the observation that cessation or restriction of visual dream imagery is invariably associated with a precisely analogous deficit in waking imagery" (Solms 1997, 131). We will discuss the relevant patterns of cortical activation in Chapter 8.

For all these reasons I think it is useful to consider dreaming to be one form of mental functioning (and cortical functioning), not a separate state, but an extreme—one end of a continuum with thought, reverie, fantasy, daydreaming. I am not claiming that dreaming is similar to waking thought.

I am noting only that there is a lot of overlap between the various forms of mental functioning. We can certainly consider dreaming to be an important and very special part of the continuum. In fact, I will discuss later ways in which dreaming may be the most creative or artistic part of our mental functioning, but it is not something that can be separated entirely from the rest of our lives.

We could say that there are several related continua rather than one continuum and I have no objection to this. In fact, Figure 5.2 shows several continua which run more or less together as we move from focused-waking thought to dreaming.

The continuum can also be looked at in a slightly different way. At the focused waking end of the continuum we are usually doing two things at once. We are split. We are thinking, calculating, plotting etc., and at the same time we are producing an image of the world around us, which we call the sensorium, that allows us to monitor what is going on around us. We may believe we are simply seeing the world as it is, but the structure of the sensorium—our visuo-spatial field—is a creation of our minds and brains. (Infants take a long time to develop their sensorium, and likewise children born blind whose sight is restored are able to see, but for a long time do not have a normally functioning sensorium) (Gregory 1997, 136-169).

When we move along the continuum toward fantasy and daydreaming—especially if we close our eyes—we sometimes re-create (imagine) a world which is usually a rough simulation of our sensorium. But we often can become so immersed in the daydream or fantasy that we forget where we are. We are no longer so definitely doing two things at once. When we go further along the continuum to dreaming, we are completely immersed in the dream's actions and are totally unaware that we are lying in bed. We do not do two things at once; we simply take part in our dream. We may do some thinking in dreams, as discussed, but it is intimately related to our dream actions. We do not think about totally different issues. We do not fantasize or daydream about something else while we are dreaming (Figure 5.3). This has been noted previously by Rechtschaffen in 1978 in his paper on "the single-mindedness and isolation of dreams," though he emphasized not so much the aspect we are illustrating in Figure 5.3, but rather the fact that in dreaming we continue "single-mindedly" for a long time on a single story or plot which we seldom do outside of dreaming. It has been noted even earlier by Samuel Taylor Coleridge: "In dreams I do not recollect that state of feeling so common when awake, of thinking on one subject and looking at another" (Auden and Kronenberger 1966, 362).

Considering dreaming to be one end of a continuum has a number of additional advantages for our thinking. For instance, it can help resolve the old debate as to whether dreams are meaningful or meaningless. There are

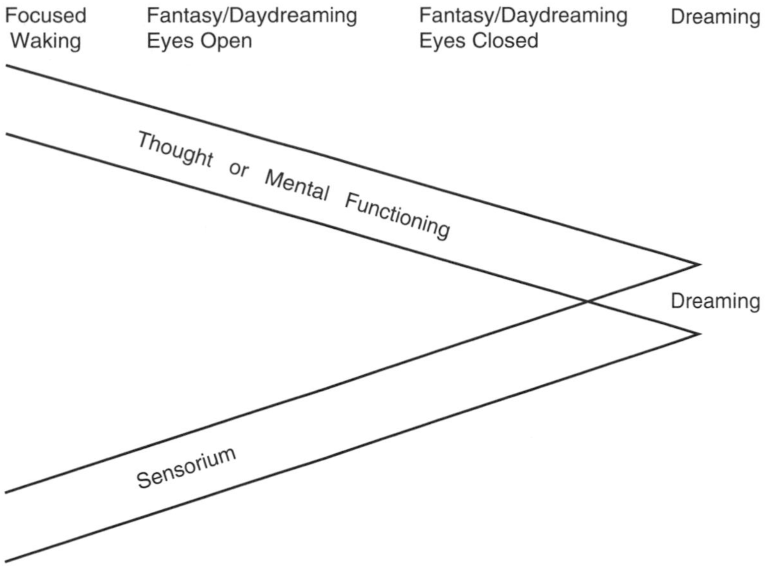

Figure 5.3 Another view of the continuum

At the focused-waking-thought end of the continuum, we are doing two things at once; we are multi-tasking. The two tasks gradually merge as we move towards dreaming.

some scientists who believe that dreams are basically meaningless random activity. Accepting the continuum, this would mean that daydreams are meaningless too, since there is so much overlap with dreams, and if daydreams, then fantasies and even thoughts would have to be called meaningless. This is an absurd conclusion, so I believe we cannot consider dreams to be meaningless. It makes more sense to accept that all parts of the continuum are meaningful, but in somewhat different ways. As we have seen, dreaming involves making connections broadly, guided by emotion, which makes dreams somewhat similar to works of art. We certainly consider works of art as meaningful, though in a different way from thoughts. (Though admittedly there are some who always declare new works of art to be meaningless!)

The continuum also allows us to relate dreaming to personality, as we shall discuss in Chapter 10. It turns out that some people prefer the focused thought end of the continuum and spend much of their time therein, while others prefer, and spend more time in, the daydreaming and dreaming part of the continuum. We have done a lot of research describing these differing types of people.

Thinking in terms of a continuum also makes it easier to understand a point made in discussing the tidal wave dream. When things are clearest, the dream pictures an emotion or an emotional concern. This is also true of much of our daydreaming, which falls next to dreaming on the continuum. Daydreams obviously picture our emotional concerns. And we have seen that a daydream under the influence of strong emotion becomes a dream or something that is scored very much like the Central Image of a dream (see above).

Finally, the continuum helps us with the difficult question of the possible function or functions of dreaming. In Chapter 11 we'll discuss a possible function relating to integration of new memories with old memory systems based on emotion. But in addition, we will note that having the entire continuum available obviously has an adaptive function (Chapter 12). It is useful to be able to think clearly, serially, at times, and at other times to imagine new possibilities, put things together in new ways etc.; in other words, to daydream and to dream.

6 Dreaming Connects. The Dreaming End of the Continuum Is Hyper-connective

Dreaming is hyper-connective. At the dreaming end of the continuum connections are made more easily than in waking, and connections are made more broadly and loosely. Dreaming avoids tightly structured, over-learned material. Thus we do not dream of the "three R's"—reading, writing, and arithmetic. The connections are not random, but guided by the dreamer's emotions.

Basically everyone agrees that dreaming is hyper-connective—that it throws together material in our minds rather loosely and broadly. Freud (1953 [1900]) used the term "condensation" to describe this connectivity. (Freud meant condensation in two senses: combining several people or places into a single one and also in the sense of reduction, reducing the length of the material, for instance combining two or more complicated thoughts into a single image or scene). Even those who consider dreaming to be more or less random nonsense agree that dreaming is hyper-connective—that a lot of stuff gets thrown together.

Examining the continuum of mental functioning, as we did in the last chapter, shows us that hyper-connectivity is not restricted to dreaming. It gradually increases as we move to the right along the continuum. Reverie and daydreaming also involve some loose thinking and broad connectivity. There is an increase of connectivity, or broad associations, in many senses towards the dreaming end of the continuum. We can discuss connections first at the level of everyday dream content—settings, people, and so on. Here, hyper-connectivity means loose associations or combinations and condensations.

It also involves metaphor—see Chapter 7. We will later try to understand these connections in terms of models of brain activity ("connectionist nets") and finally try to examine actual connections between neurons or groups of neurons in the cortex.

It is not easy to study this broad connectivity or loose association experimentally, since the subject under study is asleep at the time. One possibility is to test someone who has just been awakened from REM sleep—thus probably has just been dreaming—to see whether mental functioning is different from awakenings at other times. I did one study some years ago (unpublished), in which we asked participants to do a word association task after awakening from REM sleep or NREM sleep. The hypothesis was that after REM sleep, when the participants had presumably been dreaming, their minds might continue in the broad or loose associative mode of the dream. In other words, they would be in a different state after awakening from REM sleep than from NREM sleep. We obtained some positive results in line with the hypothesis, but the methodology was difficult. The chief problem was that some of the participants turned out to be intermittently asleep (in Stage 1 or 2) by EEG criteria while they were performing the word association tasks, which made it difficult to interpret the results.

Fiss, Klein, and Bokert (1966), along the same lines, reported that waking fantasy was more "unlikely" and "imagistic" after awakenings from REM as compared to NREM-sleep. More recently, Stickgold and colleagues (1999) performed a similar study much more elegantly, comparing associative thinking after awakenings from REM sleep versus awakenings from NREM sleep. They used a methodology involving "semantic priming." One word called a prime was presented briefly followed by a "target," which was either a word or non-word. The task was simply to decide whether the target was a word. This is easiest when the target is closely related to the prime (e.g. table-chair) and more difficult if weakly related (e.g. table-elements). They found that weakly related targets were more rapidly identified after REM awakenings as compared to NREM awakenings.

On one level, one can examine one's own dreams or any collection of dreams and see hyper-connectivity or condensation very easily. As a simple example, New York City and Boston are distinct separate places in my waking thoughts, but my dreams often put me in a city that's part Boston and part New York. A large room or lecture hall often combines features of several rooms I know or have worked in. And we all sometimes dream of one person who has features of several people we know.

These connections can often produce something new or at least show us something new, if we're willing to pay attention. I have heard the following dream, in one form or another, from six different women over the years: "I was dreaming about my boyfriend 'Jim,' and then he turned into my father."

Or sometimes the dream goes "I was dreaming about 'Jim' but then it seemed I was dreaming about my father." In each of these six cases, I did not make any comment, but simply let the woman continue: "When I woke up the next morning, I realized that indeed 'Jim' is very much like my father in many ways. He is very smart, he is stubborn, he needs to have his own way, he never listens to me, etc. (slightly different characteristics in each case), but, here's something amazing: *I never noticed that until I had this dream*." This last comment, made in one form or another by each of these women, is extremely significant. It indicates that while awake, in our focused-waking mode, we keep "Jim" in one region or compartment of our mind/brains and father in a different compartment. It takes a dream, or maybe occasionally a daydream, to cross the boundary and show us the obvious similarities.

In this way dreams can be important in our self-knowledge, even without any therapy or official "dream interpretation." In fact, I have suggested that dreaming may function in our minds somewhat the way psychotherapy does. Both in dreaming and in psychotherapy we are "making connections in a safe place" (Hartmann 1995).

Overall, dreaming appears to be hyper-connective. It makes connections broadly and loosely, in emotionally important areas. Dreaming tends to avoid the closely-knit, over-learned activities we spend our time on while awake, such as reading and writing. My collaborators and I conducted two related studies to examine our impression that we do not dream of the "three R's" (reading, writing, and arithmetic) (Hartmann 2000).

In the first study we simply examined a total of 456 dreams available from a number of studies—about half from men and half from women. Each dream was read independently by two judges who were given a sheet with three columns for scoring, asking them to score each written dream for any instance of (1) reading word-for-word, more than one or two words, (2) writing or typing word-for-word—more than one or two words, or (3) calculating or doing arithmetic.

The results showed exact agreement between the scores on all of the 456 dreams. The judges agreed that there were no instances of reading, no instances of writing or typing, and only one probable instance of calculating.

The second study involved a questionnaire sent to 400 members of the International Association for the Study of Dreams. These were people interested in dreams, and almost always with good recall of their dreams. First, each respondent was asked to estimate on a five-point scale how frequently he or she recalled engaging in the activities of reading, writing, typing, or calculating in their dreams and were later also asked how much time they spent on each of these activities during their waking lives. In brief, the four activities were given very low scores for recall. For each of the four activities, close to 95 percent of the respondents said that they "never" or "hardly ever" engaged in it. And yet these were very common waking activities. On the average, the respondents reported spending 150 minutes per day reading, 204 minutes writing/typing, and 23 minutes calculating.

Since we could not be sure of the individual meanings of a response such as "hardly ever," the questionnaire also addressed this subject in a different way. Each respondent was asked to rate the relative prominence of six activities in dreams as opposed to waking life. The activities were walking, writing, talking with friends, reading, sexual activity, and typing. The three control activities (walking, talking with friends, and sexual activity) were chosen as activities quite different from the "three R's," but also different from each other. Each of the six activities was rated by respondents on a seven-point scale rating from 1 "far more prominent in my waking life, it occurs little or not at all in my dreams" through 4 "equally prominent in my waking and dreaming life" to 7 "far more prominent in my dreaming life, it occurs little or not at all in my waking life." The results were very clear (see Figure 6.1). Reading, writing, and calculating all received very low scores, between 1-2 on the scale, whereas the three other activities were scored between 3-4, significantly higher than the "three R's," but not different from each other.

In summary, it appears that dreams are hyper-connective, making connections broadly, loosely, and emotionally, but avoiding tasks such as the "three R's." As we saw in previous chapters, dreams do not simply replay

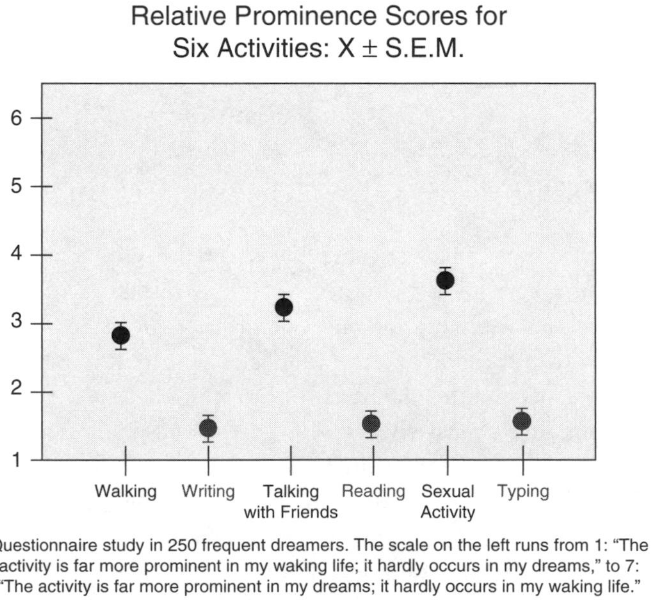
Relative Prominence Scores for
Six Activities: X ± S.E.M.
6
5
4
3
2
1
Walking
Writing
Talking with Friends
Reading
Sexual Activity
Typing
Questionnaire study in 250 frequent dreamers. The scale on the left runs from 1: "The activity is far more prominent in my waking life; it hardly occurs in my dreams," to 7: "The activity is far more prominent in my dreams; it hardly occurs in my waking life."

Figure 6.1 We do not dream of the three R's

waking material. Dreaming is creation, not replay (Chapter 4). We are always making connections. And the connections are not made randomly, but guided by emotional concerns. This is attested to by the studies we've summarized and also by a great deal of work showing predictable differences in dreaming—for instance, the repeated findings from content analysis studies that men's dreams are significantly different from women's dreams, children's dreams are different from the dreams of adolescents and adults, etc. In fact, the overall conclusion from hundreds of content analysis studies is that we basically dream about our concerns—which obviously means our emotional concerns (see Chapter 9).

So overall, dreaming is one end of a continuum. At the dreaming end, connections are made more easily and more broadly, but they avoid certain areas and the connections are guided by emotion. This brings us back to point 3 of the Contemporary Theory, which we have already discussed: **The connections are not made randomly. They are guided by the emotions of the dreamer. The dream, and especially the Central Image of the dream, pictures or expresses the dreamer's emotion or emotional concerns. The more powerful the emotion, the more powerful (intense) is the Central Image.**

In the next chapters we consider in more detail what connections mean in the mind and in the brain.

7 Connection as Combination. Connection as Condensation. Connection as Metaphor. The Dream as Picture-Metaphor

I consider hyper-connectivity in dreaming, and connectivity at the entire right-hand end of the continuum as an extremely important characteristic of our mental functioning, which has not been adequately discussed and integrated. In this chapter I will start by discussing connection in terms of some simple or widely used terms, such as combination and condensation. I will also discuss cross connection and the crossing of boundaries.

I will then discuss connection in terms of creating metaphor—an essential aspect of connections in dreaming. In a broad semantic sense, making connections is metaphor. Metaphor is ubiquitous in our language and in our thought. It is especially prominent as we move along the continuum from focused-waking-thought to dreaming. Dreaming is a sea teeming with metaphor! Metaphor is not merely the noting of similarities, but using similarity to picture or explain something in simpler, more picture-able terms. Thus, something complex such as "life" or "a relationship" is often pictured as a trip by car, a journey, but the emotion determines what sort of journey is pictured. In the following chapter, we will consider connection in terms of the neurons of the cerebral cortex.

We can consider the basic concept of connectivity, or making connections, at many different levels. Connection is a multifaceted word. I will introduce a number of different words that capture some aspect of connection and I will suggest that all of them are related to dreaming. We have already discussed connection as simple blending or combination—several people being more or less combined into one dream figure, or my dreaming of a city that is both Boston and New York. The dream we discussed in which "Jim" is my father or turns into my father can also be considered as simple blending or combination.

Freud's term condensation is also a form of connection. It includes both the blending and combination above and also the fact that many underlying thoughts—which Freud called latent dream thoughts and we might call underlying emotional concerns—may be combined in a single dream image.

Connection in dreaming can also be thought of in terms of "cross connection." This is not a frequently used term, but I think it is a useful one implying a connection of two or more very distant items, usually separated by some sort of wall or boundary. The women who dreamt of "Jim" and father were indeed cross connecting. They were crossing a boundary usually present in waking thought, which separated "Jim thoughts" in one area from "father thoughts" in another.

Crossing boundaries has not been studied much in the literature on dreaming, but it is a common concept in some related fields, for instance psychological testing—especially using the Rorschach test. In the Rorschach test—considered the classic "projective" test—the patient or person being tested is shown a series of ten standardized ink blots and asked what he or she sees in each one. The test responses are then evaluated in various more-or-less systematic manners to get a picture of the person's psychology, including their unconscious material.

The Rorschach test can be extremely rich and revealing, but it is difficult to score and it is difficult to interpret, and different interpreters have not had a good record of inter-rater agreement. Thus, at present the Rorschach is used relatively little in research studies. However, it may be important for our discussion because the psychologists who use the Rorschach have introduced three different terms for responses that cross boundaries in one way or another. These are called fabulized combinations, confabulation, and contamination.

Fabulized combinations are scored when the test-taker assumes a relationship between nearby shapes or images, for instance "I see elephants dancing on a butterfly." Confabulations express a poor boundary between what is perceived and what one thinks or feels about the perception: "I see two fetuses representing good and evil." Contamination involves an inability to maintain a boundary between independent objects, events, or thoughts; therefore, objects become fused or morphed together—for example, "men with donkey heads" (Blatt, Besser, and Ford 2007; Blatt and Ritzler 1974; Rapaport, Gill, and Schafer 1945/1946).

The detailed scoring of these responses need not concern us here. These Rorschach responses indicating a crossing of boundaries are all considered to be somewhat abnormal, indicating psychopathology and even psychosis if they are frequent and severe. What I want to emphasize is that while these boundary crossings are unusual and perhaps pathological in a wide-awake person looking at an inkblot, they are actually fairly common in all of us when we are dreaming. And in fact as we saw in Chapter 5, they can occur in daydreams and fantasies as well.

But words may be leading us astray. All of these polysyllabic and complicated-sounding terms describe something that is actually quite simple in the dream. If it sounds complicated, the problem is that I am perforce using words; I am using words and often, alas, polysyllabic psychological words, to describe a dream. Our primary experiences are not words. They are more like emotions or emotional concerns. And similarly, our dreams are not words; they are usually pictures or movies based on emotion-guided connections.

Thus, going back to the first dream we discussed, it is not a matter of starting with the description: "How do you feel?" And getting an answer: "Well, I feel terrified and vulnerable in a whole lot of ways…" and then trying to translating this into an image and finally coming with a tidal wave image. Rather, it is immediate and primary: "How do you feel?" "Tidal wave." That's just the way it is. The tidal wave image actually comes closer to the underlying feeling than the verbal statement.

But in our verbal waking world, if the person actually answered "tidal wave" in words, this would not be satisfactory. The careful interlocutor would then be tempted to ask, "Well, do you mean that you're a victim of the tidal wave, or just watching it, or are you feeling that you are somewhat like a tidal wave—very powerful?" The actual pictured tidal wave dream, rather than the verbal description, describes the state and answers the questions more directly. And usually, in the tidal wave dreams after trauma, the picture makes it clear that the dreamer is a victim, "swept away by a tidal wave."

The emotion or emotional concern forms or shapes the dream image much as it does the poetic image that we discussed: "*I should have been a pair of ragged claws / Scuttling across the floors of silent seas*." But of course the poet is in the same position I am in, writing this description: s/he needs to work in words. The dream itself can be more direct: it bypasses the words and shows the ragged claws or the tidal wave directly.

We have seen how dreaming is connective, hyper-connective, and cross connective in a number of different senses. And perhaps we have used too many different words for something fairly straightforward. Therefore I'll stop introducing new terms and deal with just one more important word: *metaphor*, which is an essential way our minds make connections.

Metaphor is language that directly connects seemingly unrelated subjects. It is a figure of speech that connects two or more things. More generally, a metaphor describes a first entity as *being* or *being equal to* or *resembling* a second entity in some way. This device is known for usage in literature, especially in poetry, where with few words, emotions and associations from one context are associated with objects and entities in a different context (Wikipedia 2008).

This bringing together of things that are in some way similar is the basic mechanism of metaphor. Metaphor in the broadest sense is describing one thing in terms of another thing that is similar, but not arbitrarily. As we'll see, the second thing (sometimes called "vehicle" or "source") is simpler or easier to picture than the first; and the process is guided by emotion!

In some sense, the role of metaphor in dreams has long been known. Aristotle stated that the best dream interpreter is the one best at noting similarities. Freud and Jung constantly made use of metaphors in interpreting dreams, though they generally did not use the term metaphor.

In 1969, Montague Ullman wrote a paper titled "Dreams as metaphor in motion." He provided many examples in which the dreams appear to be metaphorically picturing an important problem or concern of the dreamers. For instance, a man was finishing an important project, shut up in his study, leaving his wife to deal with their four children. He occasionally heard his wife yell at the children. He felt worried about her temper, and also guilty that he wasn't helping out. He fell asleep and dreamt:

> *I was calling the weather bureau to ask if the hurricane was expected to hit the city that afternoon. As I was asking the question I began to feel embarrassed and guilty.*

Ullman comments on the metaphorical depiction of the wife's temper as a hurricane, along with his gradual awareness of the dreamer's guilt. Here "metaphor in motion" is another way of describing the picturing of emotion we have discussed previously. It is certainly an instance of making connections—depicting similarities—guided by emotion.

Most of us learn of metaphor only in studying language or composition. We are taught about metaphor as simply one "figure of speech," or one type of "figurative language." This teaching is unfortunate. Metaphor is not a specific figure of speech, but a whole way of thinking, of learning, of picturing. Metaphor is basically a way of noting and picturing similarity.

Metaphor is a basic foundation of our thought and mental functioning. Lakoff and his associates (1980, 1993a) have identified hundreds of common

Table 7.1 A Few of Our Many Common Conceptual Metaphors

Beliefs are locations
Change is motion
Competition is a race
Desire is hunger
Intelligence is a light source
Love (a relationship) is a journey
Morality is cleanliness
People are plants
Time is a landscape we move through

(Lakoff, 2009)

"conceptual metaphors," which we constantly use in our speech and writing without necessarily identifying them as such (see Table 7.1). Lakoff also discusses metaphors in dreams (Lakoff, 1993b). Metaphor is the way we think, and I believe it is the way we build our memory systems using emotionally based similarity.

I will argue that metaphor is especially prominent at the dreaming end of the continuum. But even when we are wide awake, speaking or writing, in a focused-waking mode, our words reveal the ubiquity of metaphor, as Lakoff and his collaborators have pointed out. For instance, we can't help discussing a relationship in terms of a vehicle in motion. "Everything is running smoothly," "things are really rolling along," or "we're in the fast lane." And then there are times when "we seem to be stuck," "it looks like a tough uphill climb," "it's a bumpy road," "we seem to be going nowhere," or "we're on the skids," "we're spinning out of control," "I think it's time to bail out."

When we are discussing an important and complex concept such as life, love, or death, we cannot help using metaphors in our speech and we do so even more in our dreams. Here's a dream I've heard many times, in various versions: "I'm in a car going downhill and the brakes aren't working. I can't control the car." If I have a chance to ask questions and get to know the dreamer, it often turns out that the dreamer is concerned about a relationship in trouble. But, I hasten to add, there's no one-to-one correspondence between personal relationships and trips by car. The emotional concern is expressed by the dream, but the problem doesn't have to be a current love relationship that's in trouble. The dreamer may be thinking of his or her whole life in this way. Or, a patient in therapy may have this same dream expressing concern about the course of therapy. The underlying emotion guides the metaphor, but the problem—the matter one is concerned about—is not clear from the dream image.

The picture-metaphor in the dream, like other metaphors, can be understood as explaining or picturing something complex in simpler terms. "Life" and "love" are complex notions, difficult to picture or define precisely. A journey is simpler, and much easier to picture (to dream), though of course it captures just one facet of life or love.

To see how metaphor can work in dreams, let's try a thought experiment that I have discussed previously (Hartmann 1998/2001). Let us consider three familiar things: a truck, a car, and a personal relationship. At first glance, this seems like an absurd grouping consisting of two apples and an orange, or perhaps worse than that: two apples and a gorilla. Obviously, a car and a truck have many features in common; presumably they are mapped in our minds based on their sub-units such as engines, wheels, seats, etc. Cars and trucks also have some differences: trucks tend to be bigger, rougher, make somewhat different sounds; but there is a great deal of conceptual overlap. However, a "relationship" appears on the surface to be something entirely different. It is not a hard object like a car or truck. Nonetheless, when we think of how a relationship can be mapped in our minds, there is clearly some overlap with a car in motion. We speak of movement, speed, obstacles, starting and stopping, goals, danger of a crash, etc. (see Figure 7.1). Thus there is considerable overlap between a relationship and a car in motion and it is not surprising that a dream involving a car in motion often refers to an underlying emotional concern about a relationship.

The dream is not simply explaining something, however—replacing one concept with another, usually simpler one —as in Lakoff's "conceptual metaphors." The dream is guided by emotion, as we have seen in detail in previous chapters. The emotion chooses the image, or sometimes blends several to make a new one. We can decide to analyze the dream and trace it back to the "latent dream thoughts" involving a relationship, perhaps good in some ways but not going well now. There is some danger. Things seem a bit out of control, etc. But in making the dream, this all happens at once and the dream image is a picture of the emotional state (as we saw in the simpler case of the tidal wave). The dream image is a simpler description than the verbal attempts. "How are things going? How do you feel?" "Car going downhill, brakes not working."

In my opinion, Lakoff's well-delineated views on metaphor in general need to be amended to include the pervasive influence of emotion. He and his collaborators speak, accurately, of "conceptual metaphor," and list many examples (a few are in Table 7.1) Metaphor usually involves picturing something relatively complex or abstract or difficult in terms of something simpler or more concrete or easier to picture.

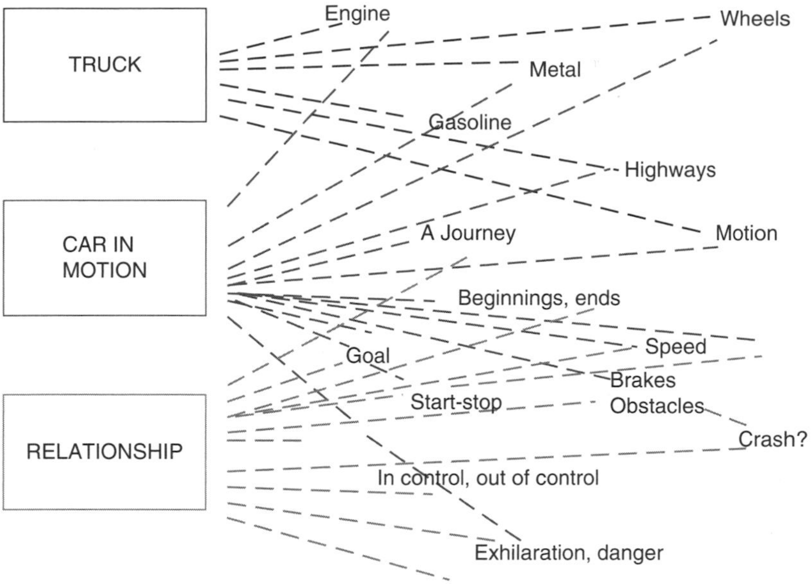

Figure 7.1 Metaphor in dreams

Assuming that any item or feature in our minds is stored in patterns representing its micro-features, there is considerable overlap between *a car* and *a truck*, and also between *a car in motion* and *a relationship*. Thus it is not surprising that when we are concerned about a personal relationship we may dream of a car in motion. Of course, this is only one possible metaphor. A *relationship* can also overlaps with, for instance, a growing plant, a competition, a battle (Hartmann 1998/2001).

Even when we are wide awake, thinking or talking, and using metaphor as we inevitably do, we say "things are rolling along," or "this relationship is off track," or "it's time to bail out;" we are not simply translating a relationship into a journey. The particular metaphor chosen obviously expresses the emotion of the thinker or speaker.

Dreams do make use of the same basic conceptual metaphors, which we use in waking life, but I suggest that at the dreaming end of the continuum the influence of emotion is even more powerful. The underlying emotion specifies or at least suggests which metaphor—which dream image—will occur.

In this sense the metaphor is a way of simplifying or explaining a complicated idea—making it easier to understand and often putting it into pictorial form, clearly influenced by emotion. For instance, there are many ways to picture a relationship. It doesn't have to be a car in motion. A relationship can sometimes be pictured as a growing plant, two plants or trees intertwined, a friendly game, a competition, or a battle. All of these images do occur in daydreams and dreams and of course in poetry, too. I suggest that the underlying emotion plays the major role in determining which of these metaphoric images will occur.

And conversely, a car in motion, in a dream or daydream, by no means always pictures a relationship. As mentioned, the same image can picture a life, a work in progress, a course of therapy. In the next chapter we will consider metaphor in terms of overlaps in representation in cortical networks.

In dreaming, this metaphoric picturing, guided by emotion, all happens at the same time. There is no series of steps as there might be in waking thought. There is no listing of possible metaphoric images which are carefully scanned and then one of them chosen. Rather, the emotion is already present and determines the developing metaphoric image. Metaphor can be considered to be based on emotional similarity. We each develop our own metaphors based on our individual emotional-biased memories.

There are numerous metaphoric possibilities, and the image chosen—the particular one that appears in the dream—presumably depends on the mix of emotions and emotional concerns that are present. Thus, a given dream or dream image may often be related to a number of different emotional concerns in the patient's life.

What I'm saying about the influence of emotion is true of metaphor in general, not just in the dream. Let's examine a common group of metaphors, in spoken or written language, which is where we usually look for metaphor. What is life? Well, we have a number of common metaphors: "life is a journey, life is a plant, life is like grass,* life is like is a battle, life is (or is not) a rose garden, life is a bowl of cherries, life is a comedy," and "life is a tragedy." (Horace Walpole (1906 [1764]) wrote, "life is a comedy for those who think and a tragedy for those who feel.") These metaphors are stated as though they were truths or at least partial truths: A is B or A is like B, but obviously these are not statements of the whole truth. Some of them even contradict others. However, they each capture a bit of what life is like when we are in a particular emotional state.

Are most or all dreams metaphoric? Is the tidal wave image a metaphor? Yes, the tidal wave can be considered a metaphoric picture of the feeling state dominated by "I feel terrified, I feel vulnerable. I don't just feel a bit scared. I feel totally swept away." We do not usually consider this kind of metaphor because we are tied down by our historical use of the term as a "figure of speech." Lakoff and his collaborators have broadened our view, by

* Grammarians will note that some of the examples are technically similes rather than metaphors, but this need not concern us in examining the working of the mind. A simile is simply a metaphor that uses the word "like."

insisting that metaphor is a characteristic not only of our speech but also of our thought—the conceptual metaphor. I believe we need still further broadening: metaphor applies not only to speech and thought but to all mental processing which includes emotion and the picturing of emotion, not just thought. And metaphor especially characterizes our functioning at the dreaming end of the continuum.

A verbal metaphor simplifies by putting something complex into other, usually simpler and more pictorial words. A picture-metaphor, as in the dream, simplifies by putting the feeling-state or idea directly into an image. Putting it into words would sometimes be a difficult task and one wouldn't come up with exactly the right words. Indeed, the emotions and emotional concerns lying behind a dream image often cannot easily be put into words, as we discussed earlier. And the picture may not be a perfect "translation" either. It's more of a pictorial approximation, or part of one.

In this sense, all our Central Image examples can be thought of as metaphors. Just as the painter or poet says "if I could tell you in simple sentences, I wouldn't have had to paint the picture / write the poem," the dreamer can say "if I could tell it in words, I wouldn't have to dream it." (Or rather could say this if s/he were aware simultaneously of all his/her mental processes.)

Picturing a wish as fulfilled, which Freud claims is basic to all dreams, is in my view just one way of picturing an emotional concern. What is pictured is the situation in which the emotional concern is solved or removed. Awake, if we're very thirsty we may say, "My throat feels scratchy... I feel like I'm in a desert" or we may say, "I wish I had a glass of water." A study by Bokert (1967) compared dreams of people when they were very thirsty and when they were in a normal state. The dreams under the thirsty condition pictured all these possibilities. Some pictured wish fulfillments—I was at a bar drinking a cold beer—while others pictured the thirsty state—I was wandering in a desert. Portraying the wish as fulfilled is only one way to picture the concern. The metaphoric picturing of a concern appears to explain these dreams better than simple wish-fulfillment. I discuss wish-fulfillment in dreams and my disagreements with Freud at greater length in Hartman, 1998/2001.

A dream metaphorically pictures emotions and various emotional concerns in the person's life. Many emotions and concerns may be active and play a part in forming the dream. Thus, often there is no one true interpretation of a dream (see Chapter 13). This is not a truly new insight. There is an old story that appears in the Jewish Talmud about a man who had a striking dream. He lived near Jerusalem, which was a center of dream interpretation, but with many interpreters of different schools. This man was a bit of a skeptic so he took the same dream to a number of different interpreters. He reported: "I went to twenty-four different dream interpreters and received twenty-four different interpretations!" He adds, "... and they were all true."

When we are at the focused-waking end of the continuum we apply formal rules. We use logic or linear thinking, which we sometimes call higher-level thinking. It can also be called constrained thinking. Large portions of the cortex are constrained into acting as relatively simple measuring devices. When we are doing an arithmetic problem, we turn our cortex* into a calculator. When we are racing through the outfield to catch a fly ball, we turn our cortex* into a navigational device, to get to the right place at the right time. We apply a task, and constrain our cortical systems into whatever is needed.

At the other end of the continuum, in daydreaming and dreaming, we impose no such tasks. Activation patterns are unrestrained, free to "wander" creating images guided only by underlying emotions and the sense of what might be emotionally important. At the dreaming end of continuum, there are no imposed rules: we associate based on similarities of many kinds, which underlie what we call metaphor and picture-metaphor.

It turns out that this use of metaphoric similarity is generally how children learn—not by "rules," but by similarities. We try to teach the child rules and definitions, but these are superimposed on the background tendency to learn by similarities. A child first learning the concept of "bird," for instance, does not learn rules about wings, behavioral habits, egg laying, warm-bloodedness. Rather, the child develops an image or an archetype of a bird something like a robin. Then when deciding whether a new creature is a bird she compares it to this image of the robin in her mind to make a decision. This leads to certain typical errors in identification—for instance the fact that most children think that a bat is a bird, but may not realize that the ostrich is a bird (Gelman and Markman 1986). Our brain functioning seems to work first or most easily by similarity or metaphor. Only later, for scholarly or scientific purposes, do we learn to apply rules.

Thinking about the continuum I suggest that learning by rules is something that we do in a focused-waking thought mode, when on the biological level, the cortex is constrained into acting as a calculator or navigational device. When we relax these constraints and move toward daydreaming and dreaming, we do not make use of rules, but just as the child learns, we work by resemblance or similarity—in other words, metaphor. Our whole sense of self is built of emotion-guided memories, and I believe that dreaming plays a part in producing and structuring our memory systems (see Chapter 11).

* I am using "cortex" as shorthand for a large number of forebrain pathways involving mainly the cortex, but also sub-cortical regions – especially the limbic system.

Metaphor in Context: the Metaphor in a Story or Schema

I have emphasized the Central Image of the dream in previous chapters and the metaphoric nature of the dream image here because I consider these to be essential characteristics of dreaming and the dreaming end of the continuum. And indeed, we find that the Central Image of the dream is often the clearest picture-metaphor. But of course there is more to most dreams than a single image. The image or metaphor does not just "hang there" by itself. In most dreams it is part of a story. Most often the dream involves characters in a story, and usually, though not always, the dreamer himself is the main character. The characters are involved in a plot or story of some kind. Almost always there is movement of self or characters through space. The story has been called a schema, discussed in detail by Cavallero and Cicogna (1993) and Barcaro et al. (2002), among others.

I have not greatly emphasized this schema or story part of dreaming, because it is not specific to dreaming. It is the way our minds' work. Awake, eyes open, we act in and move through our visuo-spatial world. Eyes closed, in reverie and daydreaming, we think of or "see" ourselves moving through a similar world. Hunt (1995) has described this movement of self through space as the basic ground of our consciousness. It is the background to our mental functioning, but it is not specific to dreaming.

8 Connections in the Mind and Brain. The Biology of Dreaming. Networks in the Cerebral Cortex

What does making connections mean in the brain, especially in the cortex—the substrate for most of our mental functioning? There are changes in the regions activated, as we move from focused-waking-thought towards dreaming. More importantly, there is a probable shift in the spread of activation. Greater or faster spread of activation underlies daydreaming and especially dreaming. The neurochemistry of REM sleep facilitates this shift. We cannot yet directly study changes in connections between individual neurons, but we can approach such changes using connectionist net models.

Central to the present theory is the making of connections, guided by emotion. In the last chapter we examined making connections in a close-to-experience sense, and discussed connections in the sense of similarity, condensation, and metaphor. At the level of the brain, making connections involves connections between neurons and assemblies of neurons in the brain—especially in the cerebral cortex. We are now discussing the same event—the dream—from a different standpoint. In the last chapter we took a "top-down" approach, while in this chapter we will take a "bottom-up" approach, examining the underlying biology, and also an "in between" approach in discussing neural net modeling.

ACTIVATION OF THE CORTEX

First of all, I consider it certain that the various types of "mental functioning," we have discussed, from focused-waking-thought to dreaming, all depend on activation of the cerebral cortex (obviously with some subcortical activation as well). These are all states in which we are conscious, though we are not conscious of everything going on. Our continuum of mental functioning does **not** include states such as non-REM sleep, anesthesia, or coma—all characterized by cortical deactivation, greatly diminished or absent consciousness, and little "mental functioning."

Thus we need to examine what sort of cortical activation characterizes dreaming. One body of relevant data involves the biology of REM sleep. The discovery of REM sleep in the 1950s (Aserinsky and Kleitman 1953; Dement and Kleitman 1957) was so exciting that those of us who started work soon thereafter were satisfied to delineate REM sleep in all its bodily manifestations, and simply assume that we were studying the biology of dreaming (Hartmann 1967). It has now become evident that life is not so simple. It turns out that REM sleep can definitely occur without the experience of dreaming and the experience of dreaming can occur in a number of situations without REM sleep (see below). So, examining the biology of REM sleep is not enough. Yet our most frequent and most typical dreams do occur in REM sleep, so the patterns of cortical activation during REM sleep should obviously be relevant to dreaming. We will summarize what is known of brain activity, especially cortical activity in REM sleep, which will give us some idea of what usually underlies dreaming. We will also examine a body of neuropsychological data concerning damage to various regions of the cortex to determine under what conditions a person suffering brain damage will report cessation of the experience of dreaming. We will consider some important aspects of the neurochemistry of the cortex during REM sleep, which are important in understanding the patterns of activation. And finally, we will look at neural net models, which may allow us to better understand the patterns of activation in individual neurons and small groups of neurons.

REM Sleep

A large number of studies since 1953 have established the characteristics of REM sleep. REM sleep in humans usually occurs as four or five separate periods during the night. Total REM sleep time takes up 20–25% of total sleep time. If you want to obtain a good dream report from someone sleeping in the laboratory, the best time to awaken him/her is in REM sleep. But REM-sleep is not dreaming. It is a state of the entire body, an organismic state, different from non-REM sleep (NREM) and also different from waking (Hartmann 1965; Jouvet 1962a; Snyder 1965). Clear differences are found not only in the brain, but in the peripheral nerves and in the autonomic nervous system (resulting in different patterns of pulse, blood pressure,

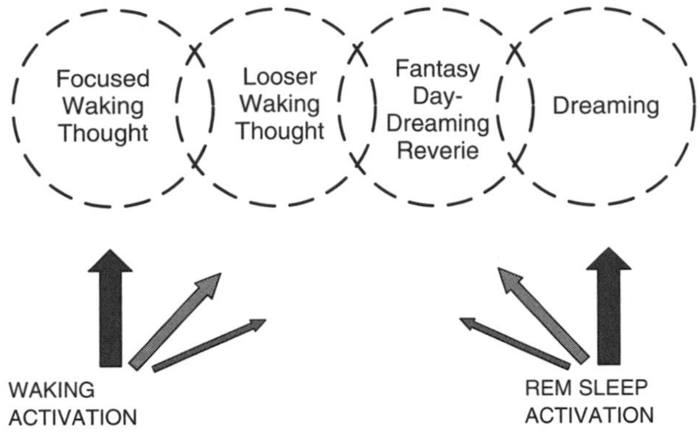

Figure 8.1 Activation of the cortex: Waking activation and REM activation (sketch)

respiratory activity, etc.), the endocrine system, the immune system—thus basically the entire body. These three basic states—waking, NREM sleep and REM sleep* are found not only in man, but in all mammals studied (with a few exceptions which need not concern us here).

There are several brainstem systems that can activate the cerebral cortex. NREM sleep is characterized by relative inactivity of these systems and thus deactivation of the cortex. Waking and REM sleep both involve activation of the cortex but somewhat different activation, produced by slightly different overlapping pathways (reviewed in Hobson 1965; Jouvet 1962a; Jouvet 1962b). The evidence suggests that various patterns of cortical activation underlie all the major forms of mental functioning we have been discussing: thought, reverie, fantasy, daydreaming, and dreaming (Figure 8.1).

Waking activation of the cortex can result in thoughts, fantasies, daydreams, and occasionally dreams or very dream-like material. Activation in REM sleep often produces a typical dream, but not always (Figure 8.1). One sometimes gets reports that involve a lot of thinking, even from REM sleep. (Awakenings from NREM sleep—characterized by relative cortical inactivation, but with some intermittent activation—often result in reports of "nothing going on," but can also sometimes produce reports of thoughts, daydream-like material, and sometimes dreamlike reports).

Recent brain imaging studies allow us to examine the cortical activation of REM sleep in more detail. These studies, using chiefly PET and fMRI technology, allow us to specify what cortical regions are more activated in

* These same three states have also been called W (waking), S (synchronized sleep), and D (desynchronized or dreaming sleep).

REM than NREM, and also what regions are more activated in REM than in waking (Braun et al. 1997; Maquet et al. 1996; Maquet et al. 2004; Nofzinger, Mintun, Wiseman, and Kupfer 1997; Sutton et al. 1996).

The results are quite complex and must be interpreted cautiously, since "activation" has different definitions depending on the technique used. Yet a few findings stand out among the many detailed brain maps produced. REM sleep is characterized by activation of brainstem regions, especially the pons, as expected from earlier studies. REM sleep also involves activation of portions of the limbic system, especially the amygdala. This is very consistent with the importance of emotion, especially negative emotion, in dreaming.

In terms of cortical activation, REM sleep (compared to NREM sleep) includes activation of the occipital cortex, especially the visual association areas, which is entirely expected and consistent with the highly visual nature of most dreams. Especially important for our present discussion, the dorsolateral prefrontal cortex (DLPFC) is deactivated in REM sleep. The DLPFC is far less active in REM sleep than in waking and it even appears to be less active in REM sleep than in NREM sleep. These differences are important since areas within the DLPFC are highly activated in waking during various executive tasks and planned activities, which involve "focused waking thought." The DLPFC is highly activated, for instance, when a person is solving problems or doing tasks, which often involve reading, writing, or calculating. This finding is very consistent with the studies we reviewed showing that these activities are almost totally absent in dreaming.

In REM sleep, although the DLPFC is inactive other parts of the frontal cortex are highly activated, especially the ventro-mesial PFC, known to be involved in emotional processing and emotional motivation. This activation is consistent with the role of emotion in dreaming, which we have discussed in previous chapters.

One other characteristic of REM sleep is highly relevant. REM sleep involves very low levels of norepinephrine at least at the cortex, which can result in increased spread of activation. This will be discussed further below.

Neuropsychology: Lesion Studies

Starting from a very different place, a series of studies of brain damage have determined what sort of cortical damage lead to reports of dreaming cessation in patients who had suffered strokes or other forms of brain injury (Solms 1997; Yu 2006). Several hundred such patients were interviewed as to their dreaming before and after the brain lesion had occurred (Solms 1997). It turned out that damage to several cortical regions—including the medial-basal PFC—was frequently associated with reports that "I stopped dreaming after it happened." ("Medial-basal PFC" is approximately equivalent to "ventro-mesial PFC" above.) Cessation of dreaming also occurred with lesions in the inferior parietal lobule of the parietal lobe. Strikingly, even quite large lesions involving the DLPFC did not produce cessation of dreaming. These results on the regions involved in the cessation of dreaming are clearly very consistent with the results on REM sleep activity.

Yu (2006) studied a larger series of patients with lesions in the ventro-mesial frontal regions. His studies confirmed that lesions in this region produced complete cessation of dreaming. These portions of the frontal lobe are also known to be involved in goal seeking behavior and in the organism's appetitive interactions with the world (Panksepp 1998). These studies demonstrate especially clearly that dreaming depends on certain kinds of cortical activation, and not simply on the presence of the organismic state of REM sleep. Cortical damage in the relevant areas produced reports of "I stopped dreaming completely after the stroke (or accident)" while REM sleep continued to occur more or less as before.

Cortical and Subcortical Regions

We have only considered the cortex in the discussion above, but obviously subcortical regions are involved as well. The data we have discussed in previous chapters, indicating that the making of connections in dreaming is guided by emotion, suggests that connections involving the limbic system—especially the amygdala—are involved. And in fact, as mentioned, strong amygdala activation is found in REM sleep.

I have already discussed briefly (Chapter 5) the patterns of activation at the cortex, which may underlie different parts of our continuum of mental functioning. There is a pattern of activation found in brain imaging studies in persons who are not actively involved in a task or problem. This has been called the "default network"—referring to the fact that it appears to be the activation pattern that the brain lapses into when it is not actively engaged in focused-waking tasks (Buckner, Andrews-Hanna, and Schacter 2008). I suggest that this default network is the activation pattern, which in various forms underlies reverie, fantasy, and daydreaming. The pattern includes relative deactivation of the DLPFC but with increased activation of other regions including the ventro-mesial frontal lobes. This pattern can be considered intermediate between the activation patterns of focused waking thought and those of REM sleep—underlying most of our dreams.

Of course, brain activation patterns are immensely complicated. Focused-waking-thought involves not only activation of the DLPFC, but of many other regions as well, including some of the posterior (occipital and parietal) regions involved in perception. This corresponds to the fact we have discussed earlier, that in focused-waking-thought our minds are split. We are aware of our environment, perceiving things through visual and other modalities, creating a sensorium—a picture of the surrounding world—and at the same time we are thinking, calculating, trying to figure out a problem (see Figure 5.3). In other words, we have a sensorium, a picture-making machine at work, and at the same time we are engaging a calculator, or navigational machine, or a thought-machine. In dreaming (or fantasy/daydream with eyes closed) the situation is simpler. We are generally in a world similar to the world of our sensorium, and we are generally acting in, or occasionally watching, a movie or story of some sort. Unexpected events may occur and odd characters appear, but we are immersed in the story. We are not (or extremely seldom) doing two things at once.

Spread of Activation Within the Cortex

More important than a shift in regions of activation, I believe, is the style of activation—the characteristics of the spread of activation—underlying the different forms of mental functioning. In the last few years, based on detailed PET, MRI, and fMRI studies, the emphasis has been on spatial localization—defining as clearly as possible what areas (what pixels) are activated under different conditions. These techniques have excellent spatial resolution but they do not have adequate temporal resolution. They do not usually help us in understanding rapid changes of activation. Magnetoencephalography (MEG), with much better temporal resolution, should elucidate this soon.

I suggest that during focused waking thought, activation will be circumscribed or limited in clearly demarcated areas, the specific area depending of course on the task being performed. Activation will turn out to be broader and less focused towards the daydreaming-and-dreaming end of the continuum. This prediction is based in part on older studies demonstrating focused activation surrounded by inhibition (called "inhibitory sharpening") produced in cortical neurons by norepinephrine (Foote, Freedman, and Oliver 1975; Woodward et al. 1979). This produces a focused beam or "searchlight" effect underlying focused-waking-thought (Hartmann 1973). Norepinephrine is found in high concentration at the cortex in waking, and is almost absent in REM sleep (Pujol et al. 1968; Jouvet 1969; Hobson, McCarley, and Wyzinski 1975; Léna et al. 2005).

Similarly, I believe that such patterns of spread of activation will differentiate people with psychological thick boundaries from those who have thin boundaries (see Chapter 10) when they are engaged in similar tasks.

Those with thick boundaries will have more circumscribed, more limited spread of activation.

Connections Between Individual Neurons. Connectionist Nets

Even with all our modern imaging techniques we cannot yet examine the individual neurons of the cortex and their patterns of activation. The cortical neurons are extremely small and there are many billions of them. The best we can do at present is to build a model of possible interactions between neuron-like units, using all the information available. One model that appears to work well is a model, or a group of models, called connectionist nets—sometimes referred to as neural nets.

Such models assume that our minds, or at least our memory systems, are built of "units" corresponding to neurons or small groups of neurons, which we cannot yet study individually. All that happens in such a network is that the "units" are activated in different patterns. The connections made more often become reinforced, a basic idea usually attributed to Hebb (1949), though a version of it may have been suggested earlier by the great neurophysiologist Santiago Ramón y Cajal. (For a detailed discussion, see Kandel 2006.) Thus, memory is understood as consisting of connection weights between large numbers of units.

In modern studies attempting to model such a net, an electrical network of multiple "units" is formed, with different connection paths between units. The connections between units are allowed to assume different strengths (connection weights). Such a network is presented with an "input" of some kind and asked to perform a task such as clearly separating aspects of the input or finding a specified sequence or pattern within the input. (These modeling studies use the computer—a tool—to simulate the neural networks, but they are not meant to imply that the brain is a computer).

Even simple connectionist net models with only a few tens or hundreds of interconnected units have shown success in modeling aspects of how humans learn simple tasks. For instance, such a net can model quite well the way we learn to form past tenses of regular and irregular English verbs (Rumelhart and McClelland 1986) or performance on the Stroop color-naming test (Cohen, Dunbar, and McClelland 1990). These models are especially convincing when they appear to learn a task in the same way children do, and make the same kinds of mistakes that children do.

These models have widespread applications and in fact a number of researchers including Cartwright (1991), Fookson and Antrobus (1992), Globus (1993), Palombo (1992), and myself (Hartmann 1998/2001) have attempted to apply aspects of connectionist net modeling to the differences between thought and dreaming. However, the connectionist net models have run into difficulty in modeling some kinds of tasks, for instance the understanding of metaphor (Kintsch 2008). Probably some modification of connectionist net modeling will be necessary.

I have previously postulated "connecting" and "reconnecting" as basic aspects of dreaming (Hartmann 1973, 1976, 1991) but without specifying any particular net mechanism. Indeed, the specific net models are still uncertain, but I hope we can maintain the elegance and simplicity of the basic assumptions of the model: the entire net is constructed of simple units and the connections between units. (This is highly consistent with the biology of the cortex.) All that occurs is a flow of activation in the nets determined by connection strengths between units; the use of the net determines and changes connection strengths so that the weights are slightly different after each activation. Memory resides in the totality of all the connection weights in the net. A given mental "event"—a specific thought, fantasy, or dream image—consists of the activation or lighting up of some widely distributed grouping of units.

Of course, the biological network in our cortex is necessarily somewhat different. It is not a randomly organized net and it is not a homogeneous, undifferentiated net. It can perhaps best be visualized as a network of nets. The network has portions in the occipital cortex which are connected more closely to the visual system, etc. and the network has "denser" portions—areas that are more "tightly woven"—involving well-rehearsed or over-learned material. The network is of course altered by experience, thus it is a trained net or an entrained net, as we shall see below.

In this sort of net, all that can happen, whether we are thinking, daydreaming, or dreaming, is the lighting up of certain patterns of units and the strengthening or weakening of the weights on certain connections; in other words we make connections all the time, or at least all the time that our cortex is activated. I suggest, however, that there is an important difference: as we have seen in previous chapters, dreaming is "hyper-connective." Dreaming involves broader and looser connections than waking thought. Figure 8.2 illustrates a small part of what I have in mind.

This is a highly simplified rendering in two dimensions of a few aspects of the net using a "spread of activation" model. I suggest that in waking there is a tendency for linear development of specific imagery usually guided by a specific task or goal. For instance, in terms of something like a house, my waking mind seldom pictures a generic house; rather it is looking for a particular house to answer a specific question: "Where did I live in 1990?" The entire pattern lights up, representing not just house but a specific house in my memory and in fact, the specific house in which I lived in 1990.

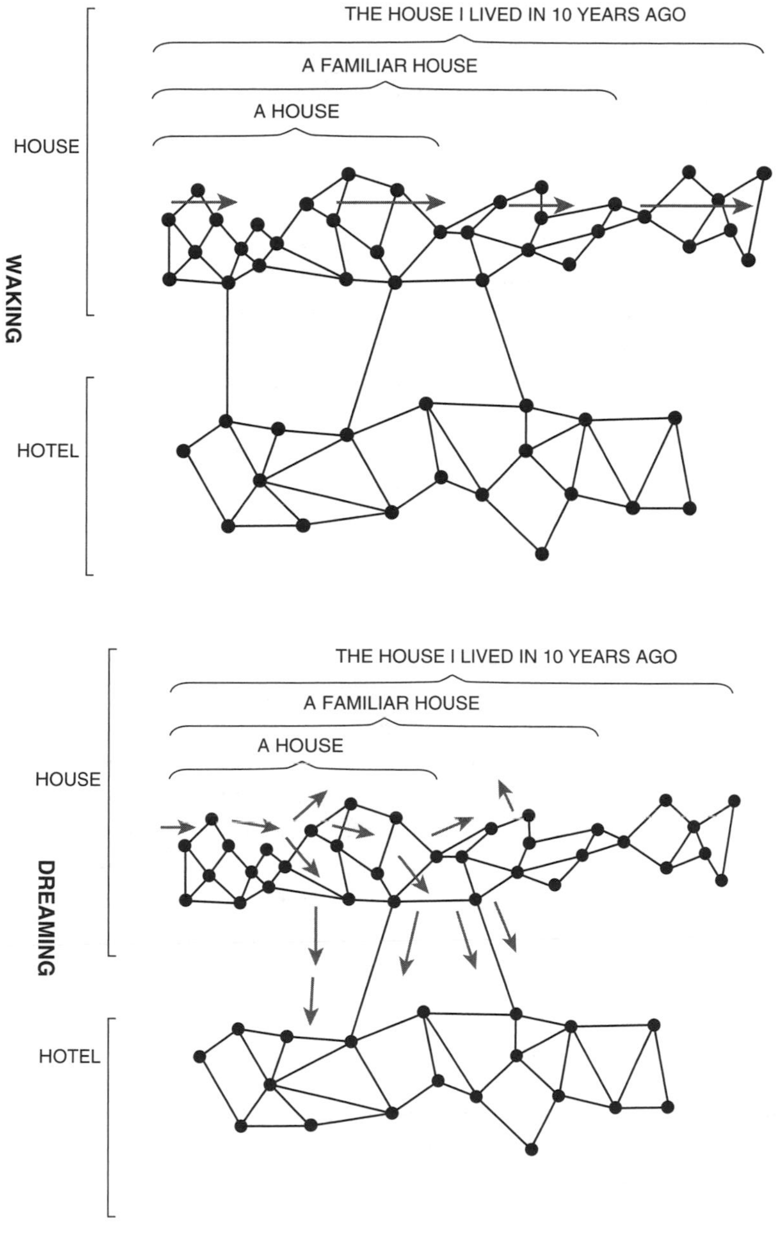

Figure 8.2 "A house" in waking (top) and in dreaming (bottom)

The activation follows a set pattern; it remains in a "groove," with relatively little "spread" as in Figure 8.2a.

In dreaming (towards the dreaming end of the continuum), I suggest the progression is less specific and less focused. The pattern representing "house" may be lit up, but then rather than only moving to a specific house, the activation process also spreads "laterally" to patterns representing other houses and other similar structures—hotels, hospitals, etc. (Figure. 8.2b). Focused-waking-thought—the waking activity that is furthest from dreaming on the continuum—tends to stay in a sort of "groove" or "rut," whereas in dreaming the activation is broader and looser.

The setting for a dream can often be a generic house or a combination of several houses. In looking over 100 of my dreams, in which I had very carefully noted details of the setting, I found that the most common settings (60%) involved a kind of generic house (or room or outdoor area); a house that was partly my house and partly a different, unknown house, a room that was partly a lobby and partly a lecture hall, etc. Freud's best known dream likewise starts with a generic setting: "A great hall…" These common "generic" settings would be scored as either "unfamiliar" or "questionable" settings in Hall and Van de Castle's content analysis (1966); their norms in students show that the sum of these two categories account for 57% of dream setting in males and 53% in females.

To supplement this quasi-anatomic view of the spread of activation, we can also consider "modes of processing:" focused-waking-thought follows a relatively serial A-B-C-D sequential mode of processing related to reaching a goal; fantasies, daydreams, and dreaming use a more parallel, unfocused, less directed mode. Many simple connectionist nets have been modeled but they can be subdivided roughly (Figure 8.3) into two categories: feed-forward nets and auto-associative nets. A feed-forward net consists of units in a number of "layers," which act on each other unidirectionally; interaction

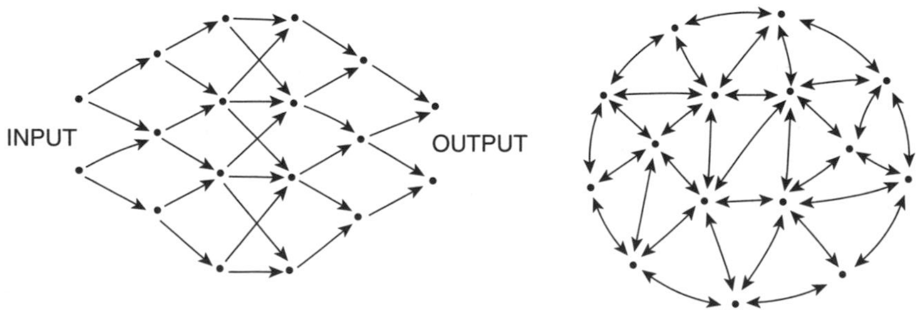

Figure 8.3 Connectionist nets: A feed-forward net (left) and an autoassociative net (right)

"flows" forward from input to output. In an auto-associative net (sometimes called an attractor net) the connections are more symmetrical; there is no clearly defined input or output; the net "settles" into more or less stable patterns. I suggest that in focused waking the net is constrained into acting relatively more as a feed-forward net, whereas in dreaming, and to some extent in fantasy and daydreaming, it functions relatively more as an auto-associative net. The patterns of activation that the net settles into underlie the particular images we see in our fantasies and dreams. The activation is influenced or guided by the underlying emotion—involving subcortical input to the cortical neurons. Certain patterns of activation, favored over time, in somewhat similar form across individuals, will become those that appear in our "typical dreams" and probably also underlie our archetypes and myths.

In these paragraphs we have been considering the same process of "broader connections" as a shift in the mode of activation rather than a shift to a different "regions" of activation.

The bringing together of material in the mind, guided by emotion, may also be understood in terms of "attractors" in the neural networks of the mind. This sort of connection or association directed by "attractors" happens all the time, but in dreaming, as we have discussed, the connections are make more broadly and loosely so that more material or more "peripheral" material gets into consciousness (For a related discussion of attractors in dreaming, see Wamsley and Antrobus 2007).

The last few pages have presented a rough sketch of the way we can understand how our minds and brains function in thought, daydreaming, and dreaming. Obviously, a great deal of work needs to be done to establish the details of this sketch or possibly to change it entirely.

9 Form and Content: The Development of Dreaming and the Content of Dreams

We are born as waking and sleeping creatures, and we are born with REM and non-REM sleep. However, our ability to dream and to recall dreams develops slowly in childhood. The ability to create fully formed dreams develops in childhood, in close parallel with the development of visuo-spatial skills and story-telling skills. Dreaming is not perception or "passive seeing." Dreaming is more like imagining and storytelling and it develops slowly along with these abilities.

Our dreams can include all sorts of ordinary and extraordinary content, but there are certain predictable regularities. Systematic studies of long series of dreams conclude that we mostly dream about our emotional concerns.

In the previous chapters we have summarized the connectivity of dreaming—the making of connections—in many senses and have followed this connection-making down to the level of connections between neurons. Now we will look at the product of these connections, the dream itself, and examine the form and content of our actual dreaming. I will not review all studies of dream form and content but will concentrate on two areas of study that are very relevant to our theory of dreaming: the formal development of dreaming in childhood and then studies of "content analysis"—the attempt to pin down in detail the elements that actually occur in the dream. I will emphasize two important and surprising findings: the very gradual and late development of "dreaming skills" in childhood, and the finding that men's (and boys') dreams have twice as many male characters as female characters, and examine what light these may shed on the Contemporary Theory of Dreaming.

THE DEVELOPMENT OF DREAMING IN CHILDHOOD

Although there are innumerable case reports of children's dreams in the clinical literature, there is only one longitudinal sleep-laboratory study of the development of dreaming across childhood. This is a study or series of studies by David Foulkes and his collaborators, who have followed individual children over a period of years (Foulkes 1982, 1999). A total of 46 children were included, most of them studied over a five-year period. One group of children started a five-year study when they were between 3 and 5 years old; another group started a five-year study when they were 8-10 years old. Thus, information was obtained on reports from REM-sleep awakenings—and also awakenings from NREM-sleep and sleep onset—from age 3 all the way to age 15.

An important finding of these studies is that the ability to dream—to produce the usual scenes and plots that most of us remember—develops surprisingly late in childhood. In Foulkes's studies, there was very little clear-cut dream recall from ages 3-5. Recall gradually increased in amount and complexity between ages 5-10. The typical dreams found in adolescents and adults involving self-representation and a series of interaction between dreamer and other characters usually appeared only around ages 7-10.

Foulkes and his group also studied the children's development in many ways, testing them repeatedly on various cognitive, verbal and motor abilities. The development of adult-type dreams was found to be related to the concurrent development of children's waking visuo-spatial abilities, measured especially by their performance on the Block Design Test and Embedded Figures Test, which are measures of visuo-spatial thinking (Foulkes et al. 1991). Foulkes considers these skills essential to the children's creative and story-telling skills.

Children with better visuo-spatial abilities on the waking test developed dreams earlier and reported more dreams. Foulkes considers the possibility that the results could be related to children's verbal abilities and ability to report dreams rather than the development of dreaming itself. However, the data do not support this view. In Foulkes's sample of children, the development of dreaming paralleled the development of visuo-spatial abilities, but not the development of verbal abilities. The highest correlations between dreaming and waking tests were always with tests such as Block Design and the Embedded Figures Test, measuring visuo-spatial abilities, not with verbal or recall abilities. Foulkes marshals a great deal of additional evidence that makes it highly unlikely that young children experienced adult-type dreams but were simply not able to report them accurately (Foulkes 1982).

In terms of our views of the focused-waking-thought to dreaming continuum, it would be important to know whether fantasy and daydreaming develop in children similarly to dreaming. Foulkes did not use the terms fantasy and daydreaming, and had no specific measures of them, but he examined "story-telling" abilities and did find similar development along with the development of dreaming. In a recent discussion, he stated that there was almost certainly a close parallel between the development of dreaming and the development of daydreaming and fantasy in the children (Foulkes, personal communication 2009).

There appears to be no solid longitudinal research on the development of daydreaming in children, though there are a great many clinical reports dealing with fantasy in the psychoanalytic and psychotherapy literature. Reviewing these briefly, my impression is that children obviously have fantasies and daydreams, sometimes very dramatic and emotional ones, but young children seldom report the detailed, movie-like, visual stories found in adolescents and adults. Most likely the ability to create detailed fantasies and daydreams develops slowly in childhood, along with the ability to create dreams.

A most important conclusion from Foulkes's detailed studies is that "dreaming is not at all a form of perception, or 'passive seeing.' It is active imagining," which is a separate function that develops slowly through the years of childhood (Foulkes, 1982, 281). "Dreaming is a creative recombination of memories and knowledge. Dreaming is not simple replay of global units from our past experience" (293). This conclusion derived from children's dreams is of course very similar to what we have concluded from our studies in adults (Chapter 4), "Dreaming is always creation, not replay."

Foulkes's results on the very gradual development of dreaming have been surprising to many, since we often hear reports of dreams—frequently nightmares—from very young children (including our own children). And there is, in fact, one small study of children's dreams (children aged 4-10) collected at home under standardized conditions (Resnick et al. 1994), which found somewhat more complex and adult-type dreams than found by Foulkes in his laboratory study. Resnick's study suggests that the laboratory setting in Foulkes's studies may have slightly inhibited or damped the telling of dreams by young children, but they do not alter Foulkes's most important finding about the development of dreaming.

I would say that some form of dreaming can certainly occur quite early. There are many reports of nightmares occurring at age 3-5, and sometimes even as early as age 1-2. But probably the young children's limited visuospatial and creative abilities do not allow them to produce a fully-formed adult-type dream. Much of what occurs in young children appears to be in the form of nightmares. My impression is that the first dream forms around powerful emotions, especially fear and vulnerability (the same two emotions we have so commonly found in adults, especially after trauma). These dreams in young children very obviously feature a Central Image guided by a strong emotion. Perhaps the most common image, based on a number of informal dream collections, is "a monster is chasing me." Sometimes it is a wild animal or some other threatening creature. Obviously, fear is prominent, though picturing of positive emotions occur too. I have heard a few dreams from very young children similar to Anna Freud's dream "I've eaten all the strawberries" which Freud reports hearing from his daughter when she was 2 years old.

Thus, I would say that some early dreaming or proto-dreaming occurs even as early as age 1-2 and certainly by age 2 -3. These dreams are hard to study systematically but appear to involve a CI – a powerful image driven by a strong emotion, often fear/terror or helplessness/vulnerability. Nightmares are very common in children everywhere, especially at age 3-5, and occur even in very peaceful non-traumatic situations. I have suggested (Hartmann 1998, 65) that all or most children feel some sense of helplessness/vulnerability when they become old enough to realize that they are not emperors of their world (as they may have supposed earlier), and that actually the world is run by large powerful creatures who may be friendly most of the time but are somewhat unpredictable and occasionally dangerous. (Isn't "a powerful sometimes dangerous creature" a good description of a monster?)

When the situation is not peaceful, the nightmares are more frequent and more frightening. Punämaki (1999, 2007) has studied Palestinian children living under constant wartime stress and found a huge incidence of nightmares: almost every 6-year old child in these studies had nightmares (age 6 was the youngest age studied).

However, these usually nightmarish dreams at age 2-6 are probably not adult types of dreams with multiple characters and interactions. The data we have reviewed above suggests that our typical adult dreams develop only gradually and slowly over the course of childhood, and that there is a similar development of fantasies, daydreams, and story-telling.

CONTENT ANALYSIS OF DREAMS—SOME MAJOR FINDINGS

Having considered the development of dreaming and the establishment of the usual visuo-spatial dream late in childhood, we can go on to examine dream content in detail to determine what elements find their way into our dreams and under what conditions. There have by now been many hundreds of research studies analyzing the content of dreams. Such research examines dream reports in great detail and quantifies the content in terms of measures such as the number of words in the report, the setting of the dream, how many characters, what types of characters, how many interactions between characters, what sort of interactions, what emotions are mentioned, etc. These studies generally use a coding system for "content analysis" first developed by Calvin Hall (1947, 1953), and systematized as the Hall–Van de Castle rating scales (Hall and Van de Castle 1966). The major studies in content analysis have been done by William Domhoff and his associates in California (for a detailed summary, see Domhoff 1996, 2003) and to some extent by others such as Inge Strauch and Barbara Meier in Switzerland (2004).

The Hall–Van de Castle system provides a very detailed look at dream content. The scoring system consists of ten categories of dream elements, most of which are then divided into subcategories for scoring. The major categories are (Domhoff 1996, 13):

Characters
Social interactions
Activities
Striving: Success and failure
Misfortunes and good fortunes
Emotions
Physical surroundings: Settings and objects
Descriptive elements
Food and eating
Elements from the past

As an example of this detailed scoring, the category "Social interactions" is divided into three subcategories: aggressive interactions, friendliness, and sexual interactions. And the subcategory aggressive interactions can be scored in eight subclasses (Domhoff 1996, 16):

A8: An aggressive act resulting in the death of a character.
A7: An aggressive act involving an attempt to harm a person physically.
A6: An aggressive act involving chasing, capturing, confining, or physically coercing another character into performing some act.
A5: An aggressive act involving the theft or destruction of possessions belonging to a character.
A4: An aggressive act in which a serious threat or accusation is made against a character.
A3: An aggressive act in which a character is rejected, exploited, controlled, or verbally coerced through such activities as dismissals, refusals, demands, disobedience, or any other type of negativistic or deceitful behavior.
A2: Aggression displayed through verbal or expressive activities like yelling at, swearing at, scowling at, or criticizing a character.

A1: A covert feeling of hostility or anger without any overt expression of anger.

Norms have been established by Domhoff's group for all of these categories of dream content (see Domhoff 1996).

I will discuss below a few of the major findings of content analysis research, and focus especially on one important and surprising finding. First of all, the consistency of dream content in a person over time has been established. A person's profile–summarizing the settings, the number of characters, the types of characters, the interactions–is quite consistent over time. In other words, if you examine a sizeable group of a person's dreams, you will find roughly the same distribution of characters, interactions, etc, as another sample of the same person's dreams (Domhoff 1996).

Domhoff's group has examined thousands of dreams and has made an important statistical contribution by determining the approximate number of dreams required to allow for reasonable statistical analysis. They have suggested that many oft-quoted studies use far too small a sample. In their studies they find that "with a real difference of twenty percentage points [on a given measure] which is about as large a difference as is generally found in dream studies, 125 observations are needed to have an 80% chance of obtaining statistical significance at the .05 level" (Domhoff 2003, 65).

Detailed studies using content analysis have established some interesting and consistent findings. For instance, children dream far more of animals than do adults; women dream more about familiar characters than do men; men have somewhat more aggression in their dreams than do women. These findings accord with our expectations and appear unsurprising.

However, there is one very consistent and surprising finding that I will discuss in more detail. This involves the difference between males and females in the sex of their dream characters. In men's dreams about two-thirds of the characters are males. In women's dreams, the characters are roughly half male and half female. This was reported first by Calvin Hall in a large group of college students (1966), and has been replicated many times (see Domhoff 1996). Interestingly, this gender difference is approximately the same among people of widely different ages, including even young children (Hall 1984). It is also found in samples from a variety of racial, ethnic, and cultural backgrounds. This single finding has been so consistent it has been referred to as "the ubiquitous gender difference" (Hall 1984; Hall and Domhoff 1963). This result must be taken seriously, though there has been no obvious explanation for it.

Of course, the close to 100 studies reporting this gender difference do not all agree precisely on the percentages, but they are all fairly close to the two thirds vs. one half ratios above. One exception discussed in detail by

Domhoff (1996) involves a careful study of Japanese dreamers (Yamanaka, Morita, and Matsumoto 1982). The Japanese men's dream characters were two-thirds male, as in other studies, but the women's dream characters were 71% female (as opposed to the expected 50%). The authors attribute this to the very sex-segregated nature of Japanese society. Though the numbers here are different, the data still show a huge difference between men and women dreamers.

I suggest that we can begin to understand this surprising, very consistent, gender difference along the following lines. Since the overall conclusion of content analysis studies is that we dream of what concerns us (our emotional concerns), we must tentatively conclude that, surprisingly, men and boys are in some important sense more concerned with other men and boys than with women and girls. No single emotion or type of interaction accounts for the findings. The data on types of interactions does suggest more aggressive interactions with other males, but more friendly interactions involving play and cooperation as well.

The Contemporary Theory of Dreaming starts from very different lines of research (reviewed in previous chapters) and clearly states that our dream imagery is driven or guided by emotions and emotional concerns. This leads to a very similar conclusion: in men the emotions and concerns that produce dream imagery more often produce imagery involving male characters—again suggesting that males are more emotionally concerned with other males than with females in some overall sense.

The sex difference in dreaming is surprising considering the general view that Mother is the most important person in our lives, and certainly the most important person in our childhood. I certainly agree with the overall importance of Mother, but I suggest that perhaps she is (on the average) too good and too reliable. She does not, in the average boy, call up the powerful and disturbing feelings that produce dream imagery or at least not as much as do the males in his life. Father may be important in this sense, but I believe that probably even more important are the many male peers, friends, and competitors that appear in the boy's life, especially at age 4-10 or so when, according to Foulkes's studies, full-fledged dreams are developing.

For boys, starting perhaps at age 4 to 6 in most cultures, there is an intense concern with peers—sometimes divided into friends and adversaries. These concerns are extremely clear if one examines stories invented by young boys and for that matter the stories invented by men that permeate our overall corpus of myths and stories. There is typically a young male hero who overcomes or conquers various obstacles and enemies (sometimes dragons, monsters, or other humans). If these enemies have a gender, they are almost always male (though there are a few prominent exceptions: the Sphinx and Grendel come to mind).

This same pattern is reflected in most of our cultural myths and stories, from the classics (The Iliad, The Odyssey, Gilgamesh, etc) to the more recent (The Lord of the Rings, the Dune series, Star Wars). The usual story involves a young, male hero, often with friends (usually male), overcoming obstacles and dangers. Women are not totally absent in these tales, but they are few and they are seldom stress-inducing. There may be a beautiful, perfect woman waiting for the hero at the end, but she seldom plays a major role in the exciting parts of the story. Occasionally there is an older woman, such as the hero's mother, or a wise old woman (grandmother?) who gives the hero advice. These women are certainly important to the hero's story, but the emotions involved are usually peaceful and constant compared to the powerful, rapidly changing, and disturbing emotions aroused by the male adversaries and sometimes also the male friends and competitors.

Thus, for the boy it appears that the powerful, disturbing, exciting emotions (the ones that lead to dream images) usually involve males. The mothers and also the beloved heroines are too good and too faithful. They do not arouse the dream-initiating emotions as much as do the males.

Possibly, this reflects the typical background of the boy's family in which his mother is obviously important but is on the average a good, caring, always helpful person. (Of course this is not always the case. Mothers who are absent in their children's lives or who have serious pathology can be very destructive. Boys growing up with such mothers may have their own serious problems that are reflected in many modern stories and novels, but these are not the usual mothers). And our typical myths and stories also reflect the boy's point of view because they were almost always imagined and written by men. All of the above may explain the predominance of male dream characters in men's dreams.

For girls, the situation is probably different. The impression one gets from novels, memoirs, and stories written by women (for instance Jane Austen, George Eliot, Virginia Woolf, and numerous moderns) is that other women are tremendously important, perhaps as important or sometimes more important than the men. Certainly competition with other women is prominent. In the past hundred years girls have appeared increasingly as heroines, but these heroines are seldom engaged chiefly in fighting male villains and monsters, as the male heroes are. So there is no reason for males to appear as predominantly in girls' dreams. In fact, in cultures where the sexes are segregated, and women's concerns are mainly about friendships and conflicts with other women, women's dreams may actually include more female than male characters as we saw in the case of the Japanese.

It will be interesting to see whether the sex ratio difference in dream characters changes as our sex roles change. So far there has been little change in the male-female ratios reported. My guess is that despite our recent movement towards gender equality, we will not see any huge change in dream characters soon, since these appear to be based on such old archetypal differences.

I believe that these speculations about myths and stories are very relevant to dreaming in view of what we concluded above in examining the development of dreams. Dreams are not a form of seeing or perceiving. Dreams are a creative activity. Dreams are active imagining. Dreams are story-telling. Thus it is hardly surprising that the dream-stories we tell ourselves are in many ways similar to the novels, sagas, and myths we have been telling ourselves. If the above arguments are correct, the content analysis data we have been reviewing is very consistent with the view of the Contemporary Theory that emotion guides our dreams, and that we dream of our emotional concerns.

The above represents my major conclusion from studies of the development of dreaming, and of content analysis of dreams. The chapter could end here. However, there are several important related issues brought up by the content analysis of dreams, which I'll take up in the next few pages.

DO DREAMS REFLECT OUR DAY-TO-DAY CONCERNS?

As we have seen, the Contemporary Theory suggests that dreaming is guided emotion and dreams reflect our emotional concerns. And indeed content analysis studies of long series of dreams support this idea (Domhoff 1996, 2003).

However, there is one body of data that appears to conflict with this view of dreams. A number of studies have examined the relationship of waking concerns—usually recorded in the evening—with the content of that night's dreams (Rados and Cartwright 1982; Roussy et al. 1996). Overall, the results have been equivocal, showing no clear relationship between waking concerns and dream content or at best a small, barely significant, relationship.

These studies could be considered to contradict major tenets of the Contemporary Theory. However, there is no real contradiction. I believe that important underlying emotions and emotional concerns influence our dreams far more than the small day-to-day concerns we are most aware of. The problem is that the day-to-day concerns are readily accessible, so people can readily mention them in interviews or questionnaires. Thus, in the studies that failed to find a relationship between waking concerns and dreams in college students, the concerns mentioned were such things as, "What shall I do this weekend or this vacation? Shall I continue seeing this boyfriend?

What courses will I take next semester?" These concerns were seldom evident in the dreams.

Over the years I have several times looked over a series of dreams of a student, and discussed them with the dreamer a few years later. From this later viewpoint the dreams seemed much more obvious. The student would say something like, "Oh yes, of course, it's so clear from the dreams. What I was really concerned about was separating from Mother and establishing my own identity, etc." But of course this was not a conscious concern which the student could have mentioned on a questionnaire at the time. In this sense, the studies of day-to-day waking concerns were not able to determine the true emotional concerns of the dreamer.

CONTINUITY VERSUS COMPENSATION

Some dream researchers have tried to organize work on dreams in terms of two competing theories: one called continuity—suggesting that dreams are basically continuous with waking life—and the other called compensation suggesting that our dreams bring up what was omitted in waking.

The idea of compensation derives from the observations of C. J. Jung on his psychoanalytic patients. The idea is that portions of the personality which are kept out of consciousness during waking emerge during dreams. In other words, dreams somehow compensate for what is lacking during waking. This suggestion by Jung is actually similar to Freud's writings on repression and the emergence in dreaming of material that is repressed during waking.

Content analysis studies certainly provide strong evidence for continuity between waking and dreaming life (Domhoff 1996). Over a period of time, the characters that occur in dreams are closely related to the characters in the dreamer's life, as are the settings, the successes, and the failures that occur. Along these lines, Domhoff (1966, 157-166) provides a fascinating content analysis of the dreams of Sigmund Freud, Carl Jung, and Franz Kafka. The results show clear quantitative differences between the dreams of these three prominent dreamers and clear consistencies in each of them between their dreams and the main themes of their lives.

In this sense "continuity" has certainly been confirmed. However, in my view the continuity vs. compensation dichotomy is not a very useful way to look at things. First of all, continuity is indubitably present in a number of senses detected by content analysis. In addition, the Contemporary Theory implies continuity of emotion. The emotion present in the person who has been traumatized continues into the night and produces the tidal wave dream, for instance.

Yet this does not rule out compensation. I believe that "compensation," in Jung's sense, certainly can occur as well, though this is not always as easy to study. In one sense, making connections and bringing material together in dreams can be thought of as compensating for the limited directed functioning of waking thought in which material is kept separate. This is demonstrated in the example of the women we mentioned earlier whose dreams combined their boyfriends and fathers.

Furthermore, I would certainly agree with Jung and Freud—in fact I think we would all agree—that we sometimes avoid (suppress or repress) certain things while we are awake and "in control." It is not surprising that in dreaming, when our connections are broader or looser, these ideas may be touched on more easily, so that material, hidden or repressed in waking, may emerge. And this is certainly a form of "compensation." And this does not necessarily involve deep-seated problems from childhood, the ones Freud would tend to emphasize. As a simple example, I have sometimes had dreams remind me of something quite ordinary that I was avoiding during waking. On two occasions it was as simple as a lecture I was supposed to give which I was not very enthusiastic about and had avoided working on until almost too late. A dream then showed me the scene or the people involved in that talk and reminded me not to push it away for too long. Obviously the thoughts about the lecture were there in my mind, and not very deeply repressed. Dreaming just brought them more clearly to my consciousness.

In these senses compensation can occur as well as continuity. The situation described above, in the students who were not aware of their deeper concerns when filling out a questionnaire, is also what so frequently occurs in psychotherapy and psychoanalysis: a deep emotion or emotional concern may be present, and may show up in dreams, at a time when the person is not (or not yet) consciously aware of it. This too is a form of compensation.

Thus, while continuity with waking life is obviously present in dreams, I can see a place for compensation as well and both are explainable in terms of the theory we have developed in the last chapters. Remembering that daydreams are not entirely different from dreams, we can also consider whether the continuity vs. compensation scheme is useful in understanding daydreams. Again, I do not find it especially useful. Obviously both are present. In the very simplest case, let's assume that we are very hungry. In this situation we know that our daydreams will deal with hunger and involve finding food, eating a meal, etc. So the concerns pictured are obviously continuous with our waking concerns, and yet we can also say that we are compensating for our waking hungry state by our daydreaming of eating. Daydreams of sex when we are sexually deprived can be considered in the same way.

BACK TO THE CONTINUUM: IS A DREAM A METEORITE OR A GEMSTONE?

Without a doubt, the large body of content analysis studies that we have mentioned tells us a great deal about dream content. I have appreciated and made use of much information from these studies. However, I would like to question a notion underlying the content analysis approach. I would like to think for a moment in terms of a geological metaphor. Do we think of a dream as a meteorite, coming from some alien place, or as an ordinary earth stone, perhaps a gemstone, when we are considering a striking or beautiful dream? The distinction is an important one in terms of the kinds of questions we will ask and the kinds of research we will do.

The meteorite metaphor underlies the views by those who consider dreams to be messages from the gods, which was a basic view of dreaming over many centuries. It also applies to those who consider dreaming a special message from an internal god or a sacred place inside us. A meteorite is a little piece of an alien planet or star and studying it can give us insight into this far-off place. Thus when a meteorite falls to Earth we immediately send it to a laboratory to have every detail of its shape, size, chemical composition, etc. precisely determined in the hopes that this will tell of something about the strange world it came from. In my opinion, the researchers doing detailed content analysis of dreams are likewise considering a dream to be a meteorite—something that must be analyzed in every detail, in terms of numbers or words, types of words, numbers of characters etc., to give us some hint about the strange planet of dreams from which the dream came.

Though I am impressed with the data collected by content analysis, I am not happy considering the dream as a meteorite. I would like to consider dreams to be more like a gemstone—an amethyst coming perhaps from an underground cliff of amethyst. When we find a gemstone we may admire it and if we are geologists we may try to discover why it occurred in a particular location, what else occurred in the same neighborhood, etc.; however, we do not send it off for detailed spectro-analysis. In other words, considering the dream to be a gemstone leads to a different sort of research—and in fact research related to our view of the focused-waking-thought to dreaming continuum. For instance, we may compare dreams, daydreams, and waking thoughts in various ways to understand the continuum better. Indeed, we have done some research of this kind, as discussed previously.

The people working on content analysis of dreams have had little interest in studying daydreams or other forms of mental functioning, and in fact Bill Domhoff once said to me in a discussion something like, "it's so much work just studying dreams, why bother with daydreams, they're much less interesting anyway." He may have been exaggerating. However, it is a fact that content analysis, using the Hall–Van de Castle system, has been applied to many thousands of dreams, but hardly ever to daydreams. (There are two small exceptions: Barrett (1979) compared dreams, daydreams, and hypnotic dreams; and a detailed study of 12 older children by Strauch and Lederbogen (1999) did use content analysis in a comparison of dreams and stimulus-induced waking fantasies.) In my view, content analysis is taking the 'meteorite' approach, considering dreams to be alien and unique, worth detailed "spectro-analysis," while daydreams are ordinary and not worth studying in detail. Obviously, I do not agree with this view.

10 Personality and Dreaming. Thick and Thin Boundaries

We are all different. We all think differently and of course we dream differently and remember dreams differently. Personality is highly relevant. One dimension of personality, called thick vs. thin boundaries, is intimately related to dreaming. People with "thin" boundaries remember more dreams, have more complex emotional dreams, and spend more time on the daydreaming and dreaming end of the continuum. The personality continuum running from very thick to very thin boundaries is closely related to the continuum of mental functioning running from focused-waking-thought to dreaming.

Dreaming, daydreaming, and thinking are done by people, and people differ in all sorts of ways. Different people think differently and they dream differently as well. This is so obvious as to hardly be worth mentioning. But are there systematic differences? Can aspects of personality be related to dreaming? Early studies suggested little relation between dreaming and measures of personality. However, it now turns out that there is a systematic difference in dream recall and dreaming style, which corresponds closely to a dimension of personality. This is worth discussing, since it suggests some correspondence in underlying organization. I shall describe in some detail the personality dimension thick vs. thin boundaries, and show that the personality continuum running from very thick to very thin boundaries is intimately related to dreaming. And in fact, it bears a close relationship to the continuum of mental functioning running from focused-waking thought to dreaming.

THE CONCEPT OF BOUNDARIES IN THE MIND—THIN AND THICK BOUNDARIES

The basic underlying notion is a fairly obvious one. No matter how we think of the content of our minds — whether we think in everyday terms of thoughts, feelings, memories; in cognitive psychology terms of perceptual, semantic and memory processes (or "modules"); or in psychoanalytic terms of ego, id, superego, defenses, etc. — we are speaking of parts, or regions or processes, which in some sense can be considered separate from one another and yet which are obviously connected. The boundaries between them are not absolute separations. The boundaries can be relatively thick or solid on the one hand, and relatively thin or permeable on the other hand.

Psychologists have discussed and explored many different aspects of boundaries, including perceptual boundaries, boundaries related to thoughts and feelings, boundaries between states of awareness or consciousness, sleep-dream-wake boundaries, boundaries related to memory, body boundaries, interpersonal boundaries, boundaries related to sexual identity and other forms of identity, group boundaries, and boundaries in opinions and judgments (see Table 10.1). All of this has been reviewed in great detail elsewhere (Hartmann 1991). The brain biology underlying boundaries is also discussed in Hartmann 2010.

The concept of thick versus thin boundaries as a personality measure becomes most clear if we examine the many kinds of boundaries, as in Table 10.1, and consider extreme examples for clarity. A person who has very thick boundaries in all senses would be someone with a sharp sense of focus, who can easily concentrate on one thing while ignoring others. This person does not experience synesthesia, keeps thoughts and feelings entirely separate ("I don't let my feelings get in the way of my thinking"), and is absolutely clear about when s/he is awake, or asleep, or dreaming, experiencing no in between states. This person has a clear sense of the separation of past, present, and future ("that was then, this is now"), has a very definite sense of space around him/herself ("this is my space, this is yours"), and has a clear sense of sexual identity ("I am a man, you are a woman, vive la différence"), group identity ("this is my group, we do such and such; other groups are totally different), and will tend to see the world in terms of black versus white, us versus them, good versus evil.

A person at the other extreme, a person with thin boundaries in all senses, may sometimes experience synesthesia, will tend to let a lot of sensory material in at once, and may have difficulty focusing on one part of the input. This person will tend to be aware of thoughts and feelings together ("I can't imagine a thought without a feeling"), and will often experience

Table 10.1 Types of Boundaries

Perceptual boundaries
Between sensory inputs
Sensory focus or "bandwidth"
Around perceptual entities
Boundaries related to thoughts and feelings
Between two thoughts or two feelings
Between thought and feeling
Around thoughts and feelings (free association)
Boundaries between states of awareness or states of consciousness
Sleep-dream-wake boundaries
Between sleep and waking
Between dreaming and waking
In and around the dream
Daydreaming
Boundaries related to play
Boundaries related to memory
Early memories
Recent memories and memory organization
Personal past
Future plans
Boundaries around oneself (body boundaries)
Barriers against stimuli
The skin as a boundary
Posture and musculature as boundaries
Personal space
Interpersonal boundaries
Boundaries between conscious and unconscious and between id, ego, and superego
Defense mechanisms as boundaries
Boundaries related to identity
Sexual identity
Age identity: Between adult and child
Constancy of identity
Group boundaries
Boundaries in organizing one's life
Boundaries in environmental preferences
Boundaries in opinion and judgments
Boundaries in decision-making and action

states of being half-awake and half-asleep, or will become deeply immersed in daydreaming or in reverie, so that sometimes the boundary between real life and fantasy may be unclear. There will be less sense of clear body boundary and personal space. This person may be very aware of the past and have it blend with the present ("I am grown-up, but in a lot of ways I'm still a child"). Similarly, this person will accept mixtures in sexual identity ("I am a man, but there's a lot of feminine in me too"). He or she will not feel solidly a member of one group, but rather be an individual taking part transiently in many groups, or perhaps a "citizen of the world." In judgments or opinions about the world, this person will tend to think in terms of shades of gray, rather than black and white ("it all depends, s/he's good in some ways and bad in others," "it's different at different times," and so on).

For some, thinking in terms of a real person or "case example" can make this clearer. Here are two real people that I have studied in detail. Chuck is a businessman in his forties. His life is well-organized and well-regulated. He follows a schedule that guides him not only through his workweek but his weekends as well. He attends church and several community meetings regularly. He thinks in black and white terms, and keeps everything in air-tight compartments. He believes that logical thought will solve any problems that come up in his life. Chuck can be emotional. He enjoys good food, he enjoys sex, he gets angry at times, but he definitely believes in keeping his emotions separate from his thinking. "My feelings just get in the way of making the right decision." He and his wife seem to get along well. They never have fights. On the other hand, they never seem very close or passionate.

Chuck is a man with thick boundaries in just about all the senses we will discuss. Chuck and I sometimes talk about people who are very different from him. For instance, some women he knows seem to be involved in their feelings all the time and do not to make clear distinctions the way he does. Though he agrees that such people may sometimes be interesting and creative, he is uncomfortable thinking about them. I ask him what image comes to mind. Chuck says, "If I were like that, I'd be a puddle on the floor."

Heather is nothing like Chuck. She plays the guitar, and she composes music. She's creative and flexible in many different ways. She does not stick to topics very well and finds herself wandering off in all sorts of directions in her conversations. It's hard for her to look something up in a book or an encyclopedia because other items nearby fascinate her, so she has to follow up on them as well. She sees the world in shades of gray: she notices gradations and appreciates various points of view, so that it's hard for her to make a clear-cut decision. Heather is unusually sensitive to sound and to bright lights. She's also emotionally sensitive and easily hurt. She remembers crying inconsolably for weeks, as a child, when a pet rabbit died. She and her boyfriend have a passionate, intense relationship. They've already broken up and reconciled three times in the year they've been together.

Heather is someone with thin boundaries and she mostly hangs around with others like herself. She considers her friends interesting, unfettered spirits. She also knows some people like Chuck. Of these, she says, "They're OK in their place, but they're kind of dull, rigid, unimaginative."

These two people are extremes on the continuum from thick to thin boundaries. Most of us are somewhere in between, and we may have a mixture of thin and thick boundaries. But I hope these two cases give a flavor of the personality dimension running from very thick to very thin, which has recently been quantified using the Boundary Questionnaire below.

The idea of thick and thin boundaries is not entirely new. There is some relationship to William James's (1907) division of people into "tough-minded empiricists" and "tender-minded rationalists." And to Kurt Lewin's (1936) diagrams of the mind as a number of regions separated by divisions of various thicknesses. Freud discussed boundaries very little but some of his followers, for instance Federn (1952), discussed boundaries in detail. There is a body of psychoanalytic literature on "ego boundaries" which definitely forms part of what we are speaking of here. The clinical psychoanalysts made no attempts to quantify boundary measures. However, researchers such as Blatt and Ritzler (1974) have made attempts, using the Rorschach test. Likewise, Fisher and Cleveland (1968) formulated two Rorschach measures called "barrier" and "penetration," which may be related to thickness of boundaries. Landis (1970) wrote a monograph in which he developed ingenious tests to quantify and measure ego boundaries. His results were not entirely clear-cut and his measures do not appear to have been widely used, but the concept is very similar to thick and thin boundaries. In recent years my collaborators and I have done considerable quantitative work on boundaries using the Boundary Questionnaire.

THE BOUNDARY QUESTIONNAIRE (BQ)

The BQ is a 138-item questionnaire which includes items about many different aspects of boundaries, divided into 12 categories (Hartmann 1989, 1991; Hartmann, Harrison, Bevis, Hurwitz, Holevas, Dawani 1987; Harrison, Hartmann, and Bevis 2005-2006). At least 10,000 persons have taken the BQ, including 2,000 in our laboratory. Table 10.2 gives some illustrative items. The response format for each question runs from '0' (= not at all) to '4' (= very much so). Approximately two-thirds of the items are phrased so that full

Table 10.2 Boundary Questionnaire: Examples of Items

Category 1: Sleep/Dream/Waking

1. When I awake in the morning, I am not sure whether I am really awake for a few minutes.
37. I spend a lot of time daydreaming, fantasizing, or in reverie.

Category 2: Unusual Experiences

61. At times I have felt as if I were coming apart.
100. I have had déjà vu experiences.

Category 3: Thoughts/Feelings/Moods

15. Sometimes I don't know whether I am thinking or feeling.
74. I can easily imagine myself to be an animal or what it might be like to be an animal.

Category 4: Childhood/Adolescence/Adult

4. I am very close to my childhood feelings.
40. I have definite plans for my future. I can lay out pretty well what I expect year by year for the next few years.

Category 5: Interpersonal

53. When I get involved with someone, we sometimes get too close.
103. I am a very open person.

Category 6: Sensitivity

6. I am very sensitive to other people's feelings.
42. I am unusually sensitive to loud noises and bright lights.

Category 7: Neat/Exact/Precise

19. I keep my desk and work table neat and well organized.
43. I am good at keeping accounts and keeping track of my money.

Category 8: Edges/Lines/Clothing

32. I like heavy, solid clothing.
44. I like stories that have a definite beginning, middle, and end.

Category 9: Opinions re Children, etc.

33. Children and adults have a lot in common. They should give themselves a chance to be together without any strict roles.
56. I think a good teacher must remain in part a child.

Category 10: Organizations

10. In an organization, everyone should have a definite place and a specific role.
58. A good relationship is one in which everything is clearly defined and spelled out.

(*continued*)

Table 10.2 *(continued)*

Category 11: Peoples/Nations/Groups
11. People of different nations are basically very much alike.
105. There are no sharp dividing lines between normal people, people with problems, and people who are considered psychotic or crazy.

Category 12: Beauty/Truth
36. Either you are telling the truth or you are lying; that's all there is to it.
76. When I am in a new situation, I try to find out precisely what is going on and what the rules are as soon as possible.

endorsement (very much so) indicates a 'thin' boundary, and the remaining items are phrased so that 'very much so' indicates a thick boundary. To score the test, the answer-values of the thick 'items' are reversed, and all of the scaled answers are added to produce a SumBound score. In a sample of 866 subjects, the correlations of SumBound with each of the 138 items were positive. The alpha reliability for the test is 0.925. All 138 items load positively on the first principal component and the Armor theta reliability (Armor 1973-4) is 0.927. Since 'agreement-set,' the tendency to agree, was controlled by reversing the scoring direction of one-third of the questions, the uniformly positive loadings attest to the idea that there is one (over-arching) principle underlying subjects' responses to all 138 questions. The BQ has good test-retest reliability over six months (*r*'s of about .77 in two samples; Funkhauser, Würmle, Comu, and Bahro 2001; Kunzendorf and Mauerer 1988-89).

An exploratory factor-analysis was done on the correlations among the 138 questions, using principal-components factor-extraction. Using Cattell's (1946) 'scree' test and subsequent interpretability as criteria, thirteen factors, accounting for 37.3% of the variance, were preserved for rotation using the Normal Varimax criterion. The 13th eigenvalue was 1.65. Items loading 0.25 or above on a given factor were regarded as belonging to it. The first 12 rotated factors were easily interpreted. The content of each factor is summarized in Table 10.3 (from Harrison, Hartmann, and Bevis 2005-2006).

To determine the stability of the factor solution, we re-factored the BQ for 364 college students in the sample only, and found an almost-identical factor-structure. Factor-loadings for this sub-sample were within 0.02 of those found for the total group (Harrison et al. 2005-2006). Another recent factor analysis on 500 students has replicated the original results with an almost identical factor structure (Zborowski, Hartmann, Newsome, and Banar 2003-2004).

Table 10.3 Summary of the Factor Analysis of the Boundary Questionnaire

Factor I, Primary Process Thinking: The 51 items in this factor (all keyed in the 'thin' boundary direction) describe a person who has many experiences of merging; of fluctuating identity; whose imagery is so vivid it is hard to distinguish from reality; who experiences the merging of objects with self and with each other. 49 of the items are keyed 'True.' Theta reliability (see Armor 1973-4) = .92.
Factor II, Preference for Explicit Boundaries: The 37 items on this factor (36 keyed in the 'thick' boundary direction) express a preference for clear borders whether it is in nation, cities, houses, pictures, stories, or relationships. A secondary emphasis is on neatness. 34 of the items are keyed 'True.' Theta = .87.
Factor III, Identification with Children: The 19 items in this factor (18 keyed 'thin') describe a person who feels, in part, like a child; identifies with children and enjoys them. All of the items are keyed 'True.' Theta = .75.
Factor IV, Fragility: The 13 items in this factor (12 keyed 'thin') express sensitivity to hurt, a difficult and complicated childhood and adolescence, fears of falling apart, and fears of being overwhelmed by interpersonal involvement. 12 keyed 'True.' Theta = .75.
Factor V, Clairvoyance: The 16 items on this factor (14 keyed 'thin') include beliefs in one's clairvoyant powers including knowing others' unexpressed thoughts and feelings, having premonitory dreams, and experiencing very vivid memories and imagery. These items also suggest a strong sense of self-identity from childhood through old age. 15 of the items are keyed 'True.' Theta = .70.
Factor VI, Openness: The 11 items on this factor (all keyed 'thin') describe a person who believes in being open to the world, trusting others, and disclosing personal experience. 10 of the 11 items are keyed 'True.' Theta = .70.
Factor VII, Organized Planfulness: The 15 items on this factor (all keyed 'thick') describe a well-organized, methodical, planful person who keeps track of everything. 13 of the questions are keyed 'True.' Theta = .67.
Factor VIII, Belief in Impenetrable Inter-group Boundaries: The 10 items on this factor (all keyed 'thick') describe a person who believes in inter-group segregation, whether a group is defined by nationality, race, age, or gender. 8 of the questions are keyed 'True.' Theta = .65.

(*continued*)

Table 10.3 *(continued)*

Factor IX, Flexibility:
The 12 items (10 keyed 'thin') in this factor have four themes: those of wishing to shape one's own space, job, life; recognizing separateness in close relationships (2 items); appreciating without analyzing (2 items); and believing that people are more the same than they are different. All 12 are keyed 'True.' Theta = .57.

Factor X, Over-involvement:
The six items in this factor (all keyed 'thin') are concerned with the difficulty of making transitions from one state to another—whether it is from being asleep to being awake, from listening to music or playing a game to ordinary states of consciousness. 5 of the 6 items are keyed 'True.' Theta = .57.

Factor XI, Preference for Simple Geometric Forms:
The 5 items in this factor (all keyed 'thick') describe a person who likes straight lines, and would like to work as a navigator or an engineer. All 5 items are keyed 'True.' Theta = .56

Factor XII, Isolation of Affect:
Two of the 5 items in this factor (all keyed 'thick') describe a person who explicitly believes in the segregation of thinking from feeling and factors rationality over emotion. 3 of the questions are keyed 'True.' Theta = .56.

Boundary scores can be obtained for each of the individual categories and factors. However, the most used measure has been the overall boundary score called SumBound, in which high numbers signify thinness. In the first 1000 subjects studied, the range has been 120-454, the mean value 271 ± 50.

WHO HAS THICK OR THIN BOUNDARIES?

A number of interesting findings have emerged as to who may be characterized by thick or thin boundaries. First, even though the items were very carefully written to have no gender bias, women consistently score significantly "thinner" (one half of a standard deviation thinner) than men, and there is also a slight age effect: older subjects score slightly thicker than younger subjects (Hartmann 1991). However, no long-term studies have been done as yet to determine how boundaries develop and change over the years within a single person.

Significantly thinner boundaries compared to control groups have been found in art students (Beal 1989; Hartmann 1991), music students and mixed groups of creative persons (Beal 1989), frequent dream recallers (Hartmann

1991; Hartmann, Elkin, and Garg 1991; Hartmann, Rosen, and Rand 1998), adults with nightmares (Hartmann 1991; Levin, Galin, and Zywiak 1991; Galvin 1993), adolescents with nightmares (Cowen and Levin 1995), "lucid dreamers" (Galvin 1993), male as well as female fashion models (Ryan, 2000), persons with unusual mystical experiences (Krippner, Wickramasekera, Wickramasekera, and Winstead 1998), and persons with a diagnosis of borderline personality disorder, schizoid personality disorder or schizotypal personality disorder (Hartmann 1991). Interestingly, although art students have much thinner boundaries than average, this is not true of established artists, who have boundary scores in the normal range (Beal 1989).

Groups that score significantly "thicker" than average on the BQ include naval officers, salespersons, lawyers, patients with a diagnosis of obsessive-compulsive personality disorder, persons suffering from "alexythymia" (Hartmann 1991), and also patients from two different sleep disorders centers with a diagnosis of sleep apnea (Hartmann 1992).

THE RELATIONSHIP OF THE BQ TO OTHER PERSONALITY MEASURES

When the BQ was first used in 1985 it appeared to be a new dimension of personality, not related to any of the then standard personality measures. Thus, there are only low and non-significant correlations between BQ and Eysenck's personality dimensions, although one study found some relationship between thin boundaries and neuroticism in a small group (Sand and Levin 1996). There were also no clear relationships to Cloninger's three dimensions of personality.

The BQ did show some relationships with MMPI scales (Hartmann 1991). In 299 subjects, relationships found were very consistent with what we had predicted on the basis of the definition of boundaries. SumBound scores correlated positively ($r = 0.32$) with the F ("atypical response") scale, and this appeared to be a valid relationship. Subjects scoring thinner on the Boundary Questionnaire did frequently report and discuss the unusual experiences described on the F scale, for instance, "I have a nightmare every few days." SumBound showed a negative relationship ($r = -0.37$) with the K scale, which measures "defensiveness," which can be considered an aspect of thick boundaries. SumBound correlated positively ($r = 0.41$) with Pa (paranoia), which is not surprising since it is accepted that Pa in normal groups measures a kind of sensitivity rather than blatant paranoia. Finally, SumBound correlated positively ($r = 0.40$) with the Mf scale in males — consistent with the view that having thin boundaries involves the ability for males to be interpersonally sensitive and to see feminine elements in themselves. Although these were highly significant correlations, all $p < .001$, the modest size of the correlation suggests that the BQ is obviously measuring something different than these individual MMPI scales.

Significant positive correlations have been reported between SumBound on the BQ and several measures of hypnotizability and suggestibility (Barrett 1989; Rader, Kunzendorf, and Carrabino 1996), as well as measures of creativity (Levin et al. 1991). An especially strong correlation ($r = 0.67$) has been found between SumBound and Tellegen's Absorption Scale (Barrett 1989). Again, these relationships were as predicted from our description of thin boundaries above.

On the Rorschach test, subjects with thinner boundaries were found to have significantly higher boundary disturbance scores, and also significantly lower form quality scores (Levin, Gilmartin, and Lamontonaro 1998-1999). Recent studies have established a relationship between thin boundaries and a number of other measures relating to personality, including certain forms of anxiety. An especially strong relationship is found between SumBound and insecure attachment (Hartmann & Zborowski 2001), measured on the Bell Object Relations and Reality Testing Inventory (Bell, Billington and Becker 1986). Thin boundaries are also positively related to measures of increased connection-seeking, at least in women (Bevis 1986). And there is a high correlation ($r = 0.51$) between thin boundaries and rated interpersonal openness in an interview study (Zborowski, Hartmann, Newsome, and Banar 2003-2004).

There have been two separate investigations relating the Boundary Questionnaire to the Meyers-Briggs Personality Inventory. In both studies the most striking finding was a positive correlation (r between 0.4 and 0.5) between SumBound and "Intuition," and a somewhat smaller correlation with "Feeling" (Erhman and Oxford 1995; Barbuto and Plummer 1998, 2000).

A few preliminary studies suggested that the BQ was unrelated to Norman's basic Five-Factor structure of personality. However, the Five Factor Model has evolved and the more recent model championed by Costa and McRae (1992) includes, as one of the five dimensions, "Openness to Experience." McRae (1994) has recently reported a very high correlation ($r = 0.73$) between thinness of boundaries on the BQ (SumBound) and Openness to Experience. We have attempted to further examine this surprisingly high correlation. Indeed, the Boundary Questionnaire includes at least two items "I am a very open person" and "I am a very sensitive person" which plainly relate to items in "Openness to Experience." And in fact, factor VI of the BQ was named "openness" long before the relationship of the BQ to "Openness to Experience" was known. A detailed examination of the items in the "Openness to Experience" scale is also revealing. The items involve several aspects of boundaries, but emphasize the desirable or positive aspects of thin boundaries. For instance, "I have a lot of intellectual curiosity," "I often enjoy playing with theories or abstract ideas," and (scored negatively) "I have little interest in speculating on the nature of the universe or the human condition." Openness to Experience does *not* include any of the less attractive aspects of thin boundaries, such as feeling overwhelmed by input, vulnerability, becoming over-involved in a maladaptive way, etc. Thin Boundaries and Openness to Experience are obviously closely related, but in my opinion thick versus thin boundaries represents a broader and perhaps more useful measure since it is value-free and covers both adaptive and maladaptive features.

In this connection it is important that SumBound on the BQ shows close to zero correlation with the Marlowe-Crowne Social Desirability scale (Earle 1992). Overall, neither thin nor thick boundaries are considered more desirable. However, a careful examination of the answers and a series of interviews has convinced us that by and large people consider their own type of boundary structure as most desirable. Thus, people with very thick boundaries tend to use terms for others with thick boundaries such as "solid," "reliable," "lots of perseverance," etc., while they characterize people with thin boundaries as "flaky," "far out," "unreliable." People who themselves score very thin on the BQ speak of those with thick boundaries as "dull," "rigid," "unimaginative," while they think of those with thin boundaries as "exciting," "creative," "innovative."

BOUNDARIES AND DREAMING: DREAM RECALL FREQUENCY

Now that we have summarized so much about boundaries, it's time to relate boundaries back to our main focus: dreaming. One of the most quantifiable and most studied measures of dreaming is dream recall frequency (drf)—usually determined by a single question, such as "How often do you recall a dream?" The respondent is either asked for a numerical answer or is given a multiple-choice question (never, less than once per month, every night). In some studies participants are asked to keep a dream log for one or more weeks, writing down anything they remember each morning. Recall frequency is then calculated from these logs.

Dream recall frequency (drf) shows a clear relationship to some biological variables. For instance, it has been well established since the discovery of REM sleep in the 1950s that awakenings from REM results in higher dream recall than awakenings from NREM sleep. Likewise, age shows a definite correlation with drf—a gradual increase in drf in childhood, then a plateau, followed by a gradual decline in drf with increasing age (Foulkes 1982;

Giambra et al. 1996). And studies of gender have generally found slightly higher drf in women than in men (Giambra et al. 1996; Schredl and Piel 2003).

A number of "state" factors affect drf; for instance, stressful events usually decrease drf in men but not in women, while starting psychotherapy or psychoanalysis, or taking part in a study on dreaming increases drf (reviewed in detail by Schredl 1995; Schredl 2007).

However, it has been hard until recently to answer the question generating the most interest: "Who remembers more dreams?"— in other words the "trait" factors or personality factors that may correlate with drf. Over the years a great many studies have led to sparse and sometimes contradictory findings (for reviews see Cohen 1974a, 1974b; Schredl and Montasser 1996; Blagrove and Akehurst 2000). For instance, there is no correlation or a very inconsistent correlation between drf and Eisenck's three personality factors: extraversion, psychoticism, and neuroticism. There is no clear correlation with repression, measured in a number of ways. Two papers reviewing drf emphasize the near ubiquity of negative results on personality factors related to drf (Blagrove and Akehurst 2000; Levin, Fireman, and Rackley 2003).

Boundaries (thinness of boundaries) are the single clear exception. It has been shown repeatedly that having thin boundaries correlates with drf (Table 10.4; references in table). Significant results have been found in a number of different populations, and with different measures of drf. The overall measure of thinness of boundaries (SumBound) usually correlates with drf at $r = .20$ to $r = .50$. [I should mention that even this apparently very solid relationship, which we discuss below, has been questioned by some (Beaulieu-Prévost & Zadra 2005; Robert and Zadra 2008) on the basis that drf as usually measured is greatly influenced by "attitude towards dreams" and may not be an entirely true measure of the amount of dreaming.]

Since the BQ measures thinness of boundaries in twelve predefined categories, we reanalyzed all our data on which the BQ and drf are available (N= 1359) to determine the relationship of these categories to drf. There was a highly significant positive correlation between eleven of the twelve categories and drf (Table 10.5).

Looking at the data another way, persons who recall dreams frequently (64 persons reporting seven dreams per week or more) were compared with 69 persons who reported seldom or never recalling dreams. Results show highly significant differences ($p < .001$) between these two groups on SumBound, and also on all twelve categories of boundaries (Table 10.6) (Hartmann et al. 1991). These two groups did not show any clear-cut differences in interviews. And the two groups showed no significant differences on any of the standard MMPI scales. Thus the results cannot be explained by differences in pathology or in the personality factors picked up by the MMPI.

Table 10.4 Studies Relating Thinness of Boundaries ("SumBound") and Dream Recall Frequency.

Study	Statistic
Hartmann 1991 (N = 600)	r = .40
Hartmann et al. 1991 (N = 600) (SumBound without sleep/dream/wake questions)	r = .37
Cowen & Levin 1995 (Frequent dreamers vs. infrequent dreamers)	F= 6.6
Schredl et al. 1996	r = .26 (questionnaire) r = .29 (diary)
Schredl et al. 1999	r = .30 (questionnaire) r = .26 (diary)
Zborowski et al. 1998	r = .12
Schredl et al. 2003	r = .18
Hartmann 2005 (All available subjects as of 2005, N = 1236)	r = .29

"Thin boundaries" are positively correlated with dream recall in many studies.

Table 10.5 Correlations Between the Twelve Categories of Boundaries and Dream Recall Frequency (N = 1,359)

Category	r	p (two-tailed)
1. Sleep/wake/dream boundaries	.315	<.001
2. Unusual experiences	.248	<.001
3. Thoughts, feelings, moods	.182	<.001
4. Childhood, adolescence, adulthood	.125	<.001
5. Interpersonal	.101	<.001
6. Sensitivity	.157	<.001
7. Neat, exact, precise	.039	.151
8. Edges, lines, clothing	.137	<.001
9. Opinions about children and others	.097	<.001
10. Opinions about organizations	.082	<.003
11. Opinions about people, nations, groups	.122	<.001
12. Opinions about beauty, truth	.096	<.001

Table 10.6 A Comparison of Frequent Dreamers (Seven or More Dreams Per Week) and Non-dreamers

	Frequent Dreamers (N=64)		Nondreamers (N=69)		*t*	*p*
SumBound Total	314	(SD=60)	232	(SD=40)	9.2	<.0001
Personal Total	208	(SD=48)	142	(SD=32)	9.2	<.0001
World Total	106	(SD=17)	89	(SD=17)	5.6	<.0001
Sleep-Dream-Wake	23	(SD=13)	8	(SD=7)	8.6	<.0001
Unusual Experiences	34	(SD=13)	15	(SD=9)	9.5	<.0001
Thoughts, Feelings, Moods	33	(SD=11)	24	(SD=9)	5.7	<.0001
Child, Adolescent, Adult	13	(SD=4)	10	(SD=4)	3.3	<.01
Interpersonal	27	(SD=6)	23	(SD=6)	3.7	<.001
Sensitivity	15	(SD=3)	12	(SD=4)	4.2	<.0001
Neat, Exact, Precise	21	(SD=7)	18	(SD=6)	3.4	<.001
Edges, Lines, Clothing	41	(SD=8)	33	(SD=8)	6.3	<.0001
Opinions about Children	23	(SD=5)	20	(SD=5)	3.8	<.001
Opinions about Organizations	26	(SD=6)	22	(SD=6)	4.4	<.0001
People, Nations, Groups	38	(SD=7)	32	(SD=8)	4.5	<.0001
Beauty, Truth	19	(SD=4)	16	(SD=4)	4.1	<.0001

The BQ does involve a few questions dealing directly with sleep, waking, and dreaming, so perhaps these questions inordinately influenced the positive relationships found. To correct for this we redid the correlations, omitting any questions in the BQ dealing with any aspect of sleep, waking, dreaming, or daydreaming. This had only a minimal effect on the results: the correlation in our large overall group fell from .40 to .37 (still p <.001).

If, indeed, there is a real relationship between thinness of boundaries and drf, one can ask why the correlations reported are so moderate, accounting for only a small fraction of the total variance. One could answer, accurately but not especially helpfully, that this is unfortunately the case, with most correlations involving subjective data such as answers to questionnaires. There is simply a lot of background variability or "noise" in the system. However, we don't have to stop there. If there is simply too much "noise," we might see whether reducing the "noise" will increase the correlations. We did this in two separate ways.

One important type of "noise" inheres in the question "How often do you recall a dream?" Based on interviews with a number of these respondents, we know that most people have given little thought to their dreaming and will provide a quick guess such as "maybe once a week" or "almost never" which may bear only a slight relationship to what they would say if they had considered the question at length, or were asked to keep a dream log. A review of this point finds considerable differences between drf from a questionnaire and from a dream diary; the dream diary usually, but not always, showing slightly higher drf (Schredl 2007). (These are two different measures of drf. The diary measure may seem more solid, but drf tends to increase when one pays attention to one's dreams so the diary may have artificially increased the drf estimate).

To reduce this source of noise in the drf, we studied a group who has given a great deal of thought to their dreams—members of the International Association for the Study of Dreams. For these people, the question about drf would be one they have thought much about, and they could probably answer it more accurately. In this group (N= 42) we found a correlation of r = .60 between SumBound and drf, which fell only slightly, to = .57 when all sleep/dream/wake questions were removed from the BQ. Thus, reducing this one source of noise definitely increases the strength of the correlation.

We also attempted to reduce noise in another way. We have been studying boundaries for some years, and our large group of about two thousand respondents includes some well-defined smaller groups, including several groups of students from different colleges and also some groups we had studied specifically because we predicted that they would differ on thinness of boundaries. For instance, we have a group of naval officers who, as we expected, turned out to score relatively thick on the BQ, and several groups of art students who on the average scored relatively thin. Within each group there was of course considerable variation in SumBound and also considerable variation in drf, which was available in our records for almost all respondents. So we attempted to reduce this variability or "noise" by examining the correlation of SumBound and drf across groups, rather than across individuals, using for each group a single point representing the mean value for SumBound and for drf.

The results are in Figure 10.1, showing a surprisingly high correlation of r =.924, p <.001) between SumBound and drf. This seems almost too high to be believed, so we immediately looked for possible problems in the data. There is at least one possible confound in the data—the fact that the groups included two groups of nightmare sufferers. Some would argue that nightmare sufferers are bound to have a high drf. Actually, this is not entirely true. Nightmare suffering (distress) is not highly correlated with drf or even

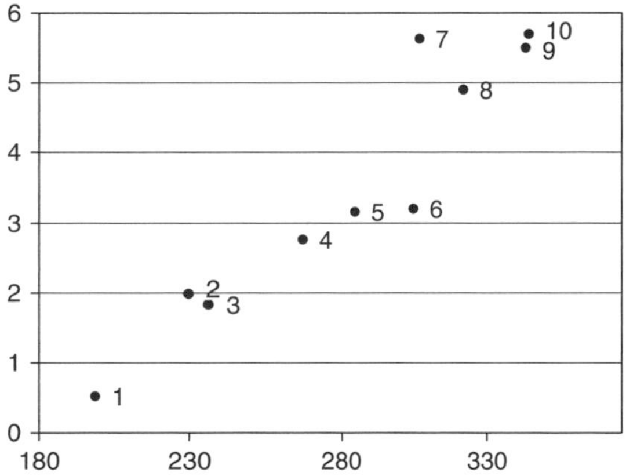

Figure 10.1 Dream recall frequency versus SumBound across groups (reprinted from Hartmann and Kunzendorf 2006-07)

The X-axis represents SumBound (thinness of boundaries), the Y-axis represents dreams reported per week. Each point is the mean value for a group (see text).

Group 1: People with a diagnosis of alexythymia, N = 5. Group 2: Sleep apnea patients at a sleep disorders center, N = 255. Group 3: Naval officers, N = 18. Group 4: College students at a New England college, N = 49. Group 5: College students at a North Carolina college, N = 197. Group 6: Music students at a New England college, N = 18. Group 7: People with nightmares, a research study, N = 12. Group 8: Members of the International Association for the Study of Dreams, N = 42. Group 9: Museum School students, New England, N = 20. Group 10: People with nightmares, another research study, N = 17. The correlation is r = .924 (p < .001).

with nightmare frequency (Belicki 1992). But even if high drf is considered likely in a nightmare sufferer group, the high SumBound scores are not obvious, but constitute an early finding of our work. In any case, to be conservative, we re- ran the correlation without the two nightmare groups, and found in the remaining eight groups a correlation of r = .971 (p <.001)—slightly higher than before! So omitting the nightmare groups made no difference in the high correlation.

In case we had introduced bias by studying only groups we had chosen as "well-defined groups," we ran another correlation, this time including all groups available to us who had data on drf, including some very mixed or ill-defined groups, such as a group of all patients seen at a New England sleep disorders center regardless of diagnosis (N = 514). Including these new groups, the correlation of SumBound and drf across all fourteen groups was r = .897 (p < .001)—almost as high as before. The fact that the correlation is somewhat lower than before is predictable, since in our effort to be inclusive we now re-introduced some of the "noise" we had tried to eliminate by using only mean values for well-defined groups.

I am not suggesting that the correlations of r = .924, or .971, or .897 should simply be accepted instead of the usual more modest correlations found across subjects. The present figure is measuring something slightly different—a correlation across groups—rather than the more usually computed correlation across individuals. Still, this different way of examining the data, which certainly reduces "noise," does suggest that there is certainly something meaningful in the SumBound vs. drf relationship. In any case, these two very different ways of reducing "noise" did result in findings which appear to strengthen the hypothesis of a solid relationship between SumBound and drf.

BOUNDARIES AND DREAM CONTENT, INCLUDING THE CENTRAL IMAGE OF THE DREAM

There have been several studies examining the relationship of SumBound or other boundary scores to various dream content measures. Hartmann, Elkin, and Garg (1991) compared ten dreams (one per person) of persons with very thick boundaries to ten dreams of persons with very thin boundaries, using a number of standard dream content measures. Dreams of the "thin" subjects turned out to be longer and were scored significantly higher on "Interaction between Characters," "Amount of Emotion," "Vividness," "Nightmare-likeness," "Dream-likeness," and "Bizarreness."

A study of 50 students who kept dream diaries (Schredl, Kleinferchner, and Gell 1996) described similar findings, using three measures of dream emotion. Thinness of boundaries was significantly correlated with intensity of dream feelings and there was a trend towards a correlation with amount of negative feeling, and also with amount of positive feeling.

A study of 80 patients at a sleep disorders center, who had filled out the BQ as well as reporting their drf (Hartmann, Rosen, and Rand 1998), investigated measures similar to those of the first study above and the findings were very similar. There was a significant positive correlation between SumBound (thinness of boundaries) and length of the dream, vividness, detail, emotionality, and nightmare-likeness.

Turning to the Central Image of the dream (Chapter 3), one study of 286 students demonstrated a clear relationship, with higher CI intensities in recent dreams reported by students with thinner boundaries (Zborowski et al. 1998). Confirming this, we found in a recent study (Hartmann and Kunzendorf 2005-06) that a group of students chosen on the basis of having thin boundaries (high SumBound scores) had higher CI intensity than thick-boundary students in their recent dreams and also in "dreams that stand out." However, we found that there was no difference in CI intensity in the earliest dream they could remember. These "earliest" dreams were reported as occurring at similar ages (6-7 years old) in the two groups. This suggests the possibility that we all had relatively intense imagery at age 6-7, but that the intensity decreases over the years in those with thick boundaries as adults, but remains high in those with thin boundaries.

THE THICK TO THIN BOUNDARY CONTINUUM AND THE FOCUSED-WAKING-THOUGHT–TO–DREAMING CONTINUUM

The material we have reviewed above clearly suggests that the thick to thin boundary continuum is closely related to the focused-waking-thought to dreaming continuum. At the focused waking thought end of our mental functioning continuum, we are making precise distinctions, we are thinking logically, we are thinking in terms of black and white; in other words we are engaging in thick-boundary functioning. Towards the other end, when we are indulging in fantasy or dreaming, we make broad and loose connections and we are functioning in a "thin boundary" manner. In fact we have already discussed how in dreaming we appear to cross boundaries more easily. For instance, for the women whose dreams involved "Jim" turning into father, we noted that in their waking thoughts "Jim" and father were kept in separate compartments, but the boundary was crossed in dreaming and the two were brought together.

The mental functioning continuum we have discussed can be thought of as a "state" continuum, which can change many times within the course

Figure 10.2 The continuum of mental functioning, related to boundaries

People with thick boundaries spend more time at the left end of the continuum (focused waking). Those with thin boundaries spend more time in and are more comfortable with the right end (day dreaming and dreaming).

of a day. The thick to thin boundary continuum has been discussed chiefly as a "trait" continuum, emphasizing that certain people have a general tendency to have thicker boundaries than others (Figure 10.2). But the two continua are obviously related. We all have thicker boundaries when we are engaged in a focused task and thinner boundaries when we are fantasizing or dreaming. And those who have thick boundaries as a "trait"—those who score thick on the BQ—prefer, and spend more time in, the focused-waking-thought end of the "state" continuum. [Aside from these daily changes in boundaries as we function in different states, boundaries can also change in more dramatic ways. For instance, under situations of stress we tend to "pull ourselves together" and our boundaries thicken; this has been called the Amoeba Principle (Hartmann 2010)].

Therefore, in many ways the two continua can be superimposed and quite likely they will turn out to refer to a similar continuum of changes in the brain. I predict that most probably this involves spread of activation in the cortex: a greater spread of activation in the cortex will be found at the fantasy/dreaming end of the continuum, and similarly, greater spread of cortical activation will be found to characterize people at the thin boundary end of the boundary continuum.

11 The Functions of Dreaming

Does dreaming have a function? None is proven, but I suggest that the emotion-guided making of new connections has an adaptive function in weaving new material into established memory, based on emotion. This is not consolidation of memory, but integration of new material with old material, guided by emotion. This can be adaptive in making subsequent new events less stressful. This integration helps establish our emotional being—our basic sense of self.

I have summarized in detail our view of the nature of dreaming—specifically that dreaming (the dreaming end of the continuum) is hyper-connective, characterized by the making of broad connections, powerfully influenced by emotions. Now we ask whether this making of connections guided by emotion is simply something that occurs during dreaming, or is it a process that has an adaptive function for the organism.

As a scientist, I have to admit that at present the functions of dreaming, if any, are unknown. (In fact, some prominent researchers doubt that dreaming has a function. William Domhoff, after reviewing in detail the evidence, or lack thereof, for a series of proposed functions, concluded, "it is highly unlikely that dreams have any adaptive function" (Domhoff 2003, 167). To me, the fact that we have not determined a function for dreaming is hardly surprising, since even the functions of sleep are not known with certainty and sleep ought to be a much easier state to understand and study.

Establishing a function is always difficult. It is hard to perform a study that will clearly prove a proposed function. And establishing a function is especially difficult for a process such as dreaming, which unlike sleep, or REM sleep, cannot be totally removed. There are many studies of REM-deprivation, and we will discuss this below insofar as it is relevant. But we cannot really deprive someone of the dreaming end of the continuum. Therefore, what follows is certainly not established fact, but rather hypothesis, though based on a large body of data.

A number of more or less plausible hypotheses have been proposed for the function of dreaming. For instance, to preserve sleep (Freud 1953 [1900]), to help solve important problems (Ullman 1959; Greenberg and Pearlman 1975), to develop the ego (Jones 1962), to develop and maintain the self (Fiss 1986), to simulate (and resolve) threats (Revonsuo 2000). Kramer (1993) has proposed a mood regulatory function and Koulack has proposed a function involving adaptation to stress (Koulack 1991; Stewart and Koulack 1993). I do not have the space to discuss these views in detail. All of them have at least some persuasive reasoning behind them, and several may well contain a kernel of truth. However, none of them are totally convincing and none have been supported by much evidence. In some cases these hypotheses choose a small aspect of dreaming and propose a function which does not appear commensurate with the ubiquity of dreaming in our lives. In my opinion, Freud's hypothesis that the function of dreaming is to preserve sleep can be placed in this category. Even if it were demonstrated unequivocally that dreaming preserves sleep (and it certainly has not been established), this would still seem insufficient—a very partial function at best. Could we really believe that this complex metaphoric emotion-guided making of mental connections that can provide insight and produce new art and science exists only as a sleeping pill? The reader interested in various views of the functions of dreaming will find a number of theories presented in Moffitt, Kramer, and Hoffmann (1993) and Barrett and McNamara (2007).

I must admit that I do not know the function of dreaming with any certainty. Nonetheless, I will make some suggestions as to a possible function, which I cannot claim to prove but which does fit with the material we have discussed in previous chapters. The suggested function is also consistent with the importance of dreaming and the large amount of time we appear to spend dreaming.

I suggest that dreaming probably does have a function—a function related to the broad emotion-guided making of connections we have discussed in detail. I see the function as a weaving in of new material—combining of new material with what is already present in memory stores (chiefly in the cortex), always guided by emotion. Emotion tells us what is important to us. In other words, I suggest that the emotion-guided making of connections not only produces the dream image but also integrates and updates our memory systems in the cortex. In explaining the dream image in previous chapters we have spoken as if the dream image were the final product—an end in itself. But it's not; rather, I suggest that it is part of the process of integration of our memory systems.

I want to make it clear that I am not speaking of a consolidation of memory, a process well studied in animals, referring to the ease of recall of specific memories such as the memory of a foot shock. I am speaking of a weaving together of old and new memories and the building of memory systems, guided by emotion.

There is no direct experimental proof for this view of function, but I believe we can see it happening if we follow long series of dreams over time. We can follow it most clearly after an acute traumatic event, when we are able to obtain a long series of dreams following the event, and a series of dreams before the event as well, for comparison. I have collected a number of long dream series of this kind. Here is what happens: the first dreams after the trauma sometimes directly portray bits of the actual events, though not always. Then the emotion (especially fear, vulnerability—see Chapters 2 and 3) is often pictured in a powerful dream such as the tidal wave dream, and then a whole series of combinations occur in which dreams appear to be connecting memories of the actual trauma, metaphoric pictures of the emotion, and pictures of similar past traumas or other related events that have some emotional relationship to the new one. Then, usually after a few months, the dreams gradually return to the pattern they had before the traumatic event.

For instance, here is a case of a definite but relatively mild trauma. A sensitive boy, fourteen years old, on a trip with his parents, was inadvertently locked into a hotel room for a day and a half. Apparently, there was no phone and no one heard him when he yelled and pounded on the doors and walls. He became extremely upset for a time before he was finally "rescued." He summarizes what happened over the next months:

> *I then had many dreams and nightmares about this event. I was always locked in, enclosed or trapped in some way but the dreams gradually changed. Sometimes I was trapped in a room like the actual one, sometimes in a very different situation. I also dreamt of being caught in a fire and of drowning in a tidal wave. Sometimes my parents were there, sometimes scenes from my childhood—scenes involving being caught or trapped—entered into the dreams. My dreams were playing with the theme of my being trapped in a room and bringing in all kinds of related stuff from my life, from stories I'd read and from my imaginings.*

He says it took four or five months for his dreams to gradually finish dealing with the traumatic event and to return to the themes they had before the incident.

Here's a situation involving a more severe trauma. This was a thirty-year-old man who lived in Oklahoma City at the time of the Federal Building bombing in 1995. One of his friends died in the bombing.

This man was a good dream recaller who wrote down his dreams and was willing to share about 200 consecutive dreams occurring before, and for a year after, the bombing. Before the date of the bombing he had a lot of dreams involving his work and his friends, and a few nightmares as well. On the day of the bombing his sleep and his dreams changed drastically. For a few nights he slept poorly and couldn't remember dreaming at all. Then for a few days he had brief dreams of simply driving to the Federal Building and sitting there in his car. Then he had similar dreams that included his driving there and looking around, noticing that the streets were empty; he was the only one there. He saw the scene very powerfully and vividly, but nothing more happened. In one dream he drove to the building, opened his car door and got out. In another dream there were other people there and a friend opened the car door for him. Then, a powerful dream of a large stadium. A police helicopter dropped a man—apparently the chief suspect in the bombing—into the stadium and the whole crowd, all 85,000 or so, went after him to kill him. Then some dreams of himself in an auditorium, feeling very uncomfortable. He was being grilled—questioned—by people up on the podium. Then dreams of being chased by gangsters, and especially of a friend being hurt by gangsters. Dreams of a Ryder truck, the same kind used in the bombing, coming to his house. Dreams of storm clouds, violent whirlwinds, many kinds of danger. Dreams of fighting. Dreams that incorporated fights and conflicts from his childhood along with recent scenes related to the bombing. Almost all the dreams had very powerful images, usually images involving danger. Many of the dreams clearly pictured his emotions, including especially terror, vulnerability, and anger.

Only very gradually, about five to eight months after the bombing, did the violent themes start to subside. His dreams gradually calmed down, with more dreams of friends and girlfriends, concerns about his work, etc., and with less powerful images. (All his dreams were actually scored for Central Image Intensity, using the scoring discussed in Chapter 3. The intensity scores were very high in the months after the bombing and then gradually decreased back to their pre-bombing levels over the subsequent year.)

Here's another case. A 40-year-old man, who had also been recording his dreams for years, provided a series of 100 dreams before and after the death of his much-loved mother. He reported some powerful dreams in the first weeks, with striking images obviously relating to the death. These are the first two dreams he recorded after her death:

> *A mountain has split. A large round hill or mountain has split into two pieces, and there are arrangements I have to make to take care of it.*

> *I'm walking around in a large park. A huge tree has fallen down, maybe a hollow tree. A man tells me he saw it fall. Then it happens*

again, in front of me. I approach the tree, see it shake a bit. I run away, then run back to it. I watch it fall again.

Then many other powerful images. He dreams of large strange-looking silver rings, being in prison, travels to strange places. He dreams of a beautiful six-year-old girl running over the water, sort of walking on water. Startling, unusual images, not common in his previous dreams. Over the next months, images of his work, his family, his ex-wife, his current girlfriend, find their way into his dreams and the imagery becomes gradually less dramatic, less intense, and more familiar. It takes some months for these elements of his life to become the most common elements of his dreams, as they had been before his mother's death. Again the dreams were scored for CIs. CI intensity scores were very high in the weeks after his mother's death and then gradually returned to their previous levels. The CI intensity scores in these two cases clearly mirror the power of the emotion, as we have discussed. And the images, combining recent events, past related events, and metaphoric pictures of the emotion, suggest a weaving in or integration.

In these three cases involving a single traumatic event, one can trace a gradual "playing with" and "weaving in" of the traumatic material. I suggest that this happens all the time, but is harder to follow when there is no single "marker" event such as a trauma or a death.

I suggest that this connecting and combining process after trauma can be useful (adaptive) in several related ways. First of all, once these connections are made, the material is not so frightening. The dreamer no longer feels "this is the most horrible thing that has ever happened to anyone; how can I survive this?" but rather notes that this experience is "somewhat like ... not too different from ... reminds me of ..." This quieting effect can be adaptive in itself. In addition, the connections between such a traumatic event (or any stressful event) and the existing memory stores will be useful in making a subsequent trauma less distressing if it should happen again or if something similar should happen.

Dreams after trauma, which we have followed so carefully, represent an extreme case, and perhaps the simplest case, in which we can see most easily what is going on. Thinking biologically, I consider it likely that "weaving-in" and integrating new material is the brain's way of extending and developing memory systems, especially long-term memory systems in the cortex. (But of course involving subcortical connections to the hippocampus and amygdala as well.) The fact we have emphasized earlier, that emotion plays a dominant role in guiding the dream, is also important functionally. It is adaptive for our memory stores to be organized according to what is truly important for us. And this means guided by emotion and organized according to which emotions are involved. In other words, emotion guides not only the dream imagery, but also the organization of memory.

We know from many sources that memory is not a simple filing cabinet from which the same memory can be pulled repeatedly, unchanged. Rather, memory is always being restructured or re-contextualized. I suggest that dreaming plays a prominent role in this restructuring, especially in weaving-in new material. In this general sense, I suggest that dreaming functions in integrating new experience into memory, guided by emotion, which is what makes up our personal sense of meaning and sense of self (see below).

THE FUNCTIONS OF REM SLEEP AND THE FUNCTIONS OF DREAMING

Since so much dreaming occurs during REM sleep, we would expect that these postulated functions of dreaming should be closely related to the functions of REM sleep. In fact, since the cortical activation of REM sleep is the cortical activation underlying the most typical dreaming, I would say that the functions of dreaming we have discussed are the functions of the cortical activation of REM sleep.

Though no function of REM sleep is firmly established, I will discuss several well-known evidence-supported proposed functions, which can be related to the functions of dreaming I have proposed above. First, there is a function proposed by Roffwarg, Muzio, and Dement in 1966. Based on the extremely high amounts of REM sleep found early in life in most mammals, these authors proposed that in a broad sense REM functions to develop the central nervous system. Indeed, REM sleep appears to be highest when there is most rapid development of the CNS just after birth, with a gradual decrease thereafter. This hypothesis was strengthened by later studies that showed even higher proportions of REM sleep in prematurely born guinea pigs (Astic and Jouvet-Mounier 1971). Similar findings have also been reported in the human fetus in the last trimester (Hoppenbrouwers, Ugartechea, Combs, Hodgman, Harper, and Sterman 1978) at a time of very rapid growth of the CNS.

This proposed function has always appeared reasonable, if not very specific, though little data other than the above has directly supported it. Since development of the CNS clearly implies forming new connections between neurons, this proposed function is very consistent with the proposed function of dreaming, which involves making and re-making connections, chiefly in the cortex. The functions of dreaming, above, could be considered the cortical, or "highest-level," part of the developmental function of REM sleep.

Another view of the functions of REM sleep has developed gradually in a series of reports by Rechtschaffen et al. (1983, 1989). This group conducted careful, well-controlled studies of sleep deprivation and REM sleep deprivation in rats, showing that REM deprivation for 20 days or more was lethal. The pathology leading to death appeared to involve a progressive inability to control body temperature. The rats' thermoregulatory capacity was lost, which apparently lead to their deaths. Thus, the authors suggested that REM sleep functions to maintain thermoregulation.

Thermoregulation seems a long way from weaving new material into old memory systems, but I believe they may be related in that they are both homeostatic processes. Thermoregulation is one of the mammalian body's most basic homeostatic mechanisms, while dreaming can be considered homeostasis at the level of cortical memory systems. Years ago I proposed a broad view of the functions of REM sleep based on a number of pharmacological and neurochemical studies (Hartmann 1970, 1973). I suggested that REM sleep functions to restore norepinephrine-dependent systems in the brain. Many or perhaps all homeostatic systems depend at least in part on brain norepinephrine. Therefore, I proposed that REM sleep functions to restore all the norepinephrine-dependent homeostatic systems (Hartmann 1988). These systems regulate the body's processes at different levels of the CNS. The largest or most dramatic such homeostatic mechanism is probably thermoregulation, which is regulated at a relatively "primitive" brainstem and hypothalamic level. Disturbance here is the most disruptive to the organism, and leads to the lethal results found in the REM-deprivation studies. Then there is homeostatic regulation of more subtle physiological functions including pulse, respiratory rate, blood pressure, and also various chemical and endocrine systems. (All these systems—including thermoregulation—are poorly regulated during the course of REM sleep itself (reviewed in Hartmann 1973). The idea is that they are temporarily "under repair" during REM sleep).

I suggest that dreaming, representing REM activity at the cortical and limbic system level, can be considered part of this homeostatic series. Dreaming can be considered homeostatic regulation occurring chiefly at the cortical level. This can be seen as an immediate "calming of the storm" after a traumatic or emotionally disturbing event (Hartmann 1998/2001). In the longer term, the idea is that the new material is integrated into memory systems in the cortex. After such integration, a similar stress-inducing event will seem at least somewhat familiar and will not produce as much disruption. In this sense the functions proposed for dreaming fit well into the series of functions proposed for REM sleep—all maintaining or restoring homeostasis.

I want to emphasize that the emotion-guided building of memory systems I am speaking of is not memory consolidation, which has been proposed as one function of sleep and of REM sleep (Ellenbogen, Payne, and Stickgold 2006; Poe, Nitz, McNaughton, and Barnes 2000). Memory consolidation is a process well studied in animals. It refers to a "stamping in" of a memory, making it easier to recall on later testing. We are speaking not of stamping in, but weaving in, or interweaving, which means giving a memory more associations and richer connections, not making it easier to recall.[1] We cannot see the individual neurons and synapses, but we are talking about some form of increased connectivity—richer connections—in the cortex. The process may also include increased "loops of complexity" in limbic-cortical systems, guided by emotion.

There are recent research studies, in animals and humans, indicating that REM sleep plays a role in memory (and that non-REM likewise plays a role, though a somewhat different one) (Stickgold 2005; Walker and Stickgold 2006). The details are still developing, but REM sleep appears to play a role especially in learning procedural tasks, which require reorganization at the cortical level. This is consistent with the present proposals. One very recent study finds that a nap including REM sleep improved performance on the Remote Associates Test (a measure of creativity) after priming, compared to a nap without REM sleep and other control conditions (Cai, Mednick, Harrison, Kanady, and Mednick 2009). This suggests a role for REM sleep not so much in consolidating memory, but in improving creativity.

Our proposed theory of functions would predict that REM sleep would be especially important to tasks involving emotions. There is one relevant report showing that emotional material is better remembered after three hours of sleep than after three hours of waking, and best after three hour of "late sleep," which contains most REM sleep (Wagner, Gais, and Born 2001). Also relevant may be a study by Payne et al (2008) which showed that periods of sleep (though not necessarily REM sleep) improved memory of negative objects in material to be recalled. Carlyle Smith (2010) has recently reviewed experimental studies by his group and others on sleep and memory and concludes that REM sleep is especially important in the processing of emotionally charged memories. These results are obviously consistent with the functions of dreaming outlined here.

MEMORY SYSTEMS BASED ON EMOTION

I have tried to state this proposed memory–processing function in several different ways. In one article I called it "taking new experiences, especially if

[1] In fact PTSD, which involves the failure of these memory-integrating systems, is associated with extremely good recall of the traumatic event.

they are traumatic or emotional, and gradually connecting them, multiply connecting them into existing memory" (Hartmann 2007). In another article I spoke of "weaving in" new material and I suggested, "This process helps build memory systems based on what is emotionally important" (Hartmann 2008b). Whatever words describe it, we are not talking about consolidation of memory or a small detail of memory formation. We are discussing a building of memory systems based on meaningful similarity (metaphor) guided by emotion. Such a memory system is basic to our entire selves, to what makes us meaningful unique individuals.

There is little question that emotion and emotional events influence the brain and its memory systems. As one simple example, it has been shown that different rabbits produce very different brain activation patterns when exposed to a given smell, and the activation patterns are related to the individual rabbit's previous emotional experience relating to that smell (Freeman 1999). Numerous studies in humans as well as animals have demonstrated the importance of emotion at all stages of memory processing: encoding, consolidation, storage, and retrieval (LaBar and Cabeza 2000).

Theoretical views of memory, starting in very different places, also emphasize the importance of emotion. Gerald Edelman has been trying to model ways in which simple neurons can become connected into layers and maps that eventually produce our entire spectrum of mental abilities including functioning memory systems. In his multileveled model called "Neural Darwinism" he concludes that the development of memory depends on "value systems" (Edelman and Tononi 2000), which correspond roughly to our basic emotions.

The organization of memory and development of personal meaning along emotional lines has also been proposed and discussed by a number of psychoanalytic thinkers, for instance Rapaport as early as 1952, and more recently Modell in 2003, starting from their own frames of reference. For instance, Modell writes: "Emotional memories, by means of metaphoric associations, form unconscious categories that are the source of potential meaning (2003, 152)". Neither Rapaport nor Modell (nor Edelman) suggests a role for dreaming in this process. It is possible that emotion-guided restructuring of memory and creation of emotional meaning occurs constantly, day and night. However, let us remember the continuum of mental functioning we have discussed at length in previous chapters. We are always functioning somewhere on the continuum. It seems unlikely to me that we are doing much emotion-guided restructuring while engaged in a math problem, at the focused-waking-thought end of the continuum. It seems probable that the weaving-in and restructuring occurs more towards the right end of the continuum as we get away from focused-waking thought towards fantasy and dreaming.

Literary critics, coming from a very different background, also emphasize the importance of this metaphoric weaving in (integration using metaphor). Thus Cynthia Ozick (1989), writing chiefly about the use of metaphor in literature, says: "Metaphor relies on what has been experienced before and therefore transforms the strange into the familiar (280). Without metaphor… we cannot imagine the life of the Other. We cannot imagine what it is to be someone else. Metaphor is the reciprocal agent, the universalizing force that makes possible power to envision the stranger's heart (279)."

Dreaming recombines, or plays with, the material in our memory. It does this metaphorically, guided by emotion. We discussed in Chapter 7 the importance of metaphor in dream imagery and the role of emotion in choosing the appropriate metaphor. As we go through life, we each develop our own metaphors based on our emotionally important experiences and this makes us more complex and more individual. For some of us, at certain times, life may be a vigorously growing plant and love may be a smooth journey in a beautiful new car. For others, or at other times, life is a long battle and love is rolling downhill in a jalopy without brakes.

Severe trauma interferes with this emotion-guided metaphoric process. When we are traumatized our dreams become "stuck" and repetitive (as in PTSD), we fail to integrate our memories, and we do not develop new playful metaphors. We do not develop connections and loops of complexity in the cortex. Our repetitive dreams of PTSD may be disturbing in themselves, but they are the tip of an iceberg. We are stuck, and the emotion-guided metaphoric development of our entire selves stops or is badly warped, as seen in the multiple problems of PTSD that have been studied so extensively in recent years (Herman 1992; van der Kolk 1997).

I cannot claim of course that the lack of metaphoric connections in dreaming directly causes the many psychological problems of PTSD. However, it is part of the process. Disentangling cause and effect is not easy but there is some evidence (Mellman et al. 2001) indicating that after a trauma, such as an auto accident, patients who have vivid metaphoric dreams (such as tidal wave dreams) have a better result and are less likely to develop PTSD.

ADDITIONAL FUNCTIONS WHEN DREAMS ARE REMEMBERED

I suggest above that making connections, weaving new material into memory systems, guided by emotions, may be the primary function of dreaming.

It occurs whether or not a dream is remembered. But when a dream is remembered, there are secondary functions as well. For instance, the connections in the dream, once we think of them in the morning, can help us see new aspects of ourselves, or see things differently, as we have noted in the six women who dreamt of "Jim" turning into Father. Two of these women did re-evaluate their relationship with "Jim" after thinking about their dreams. And of course the new discoveries and works of art based on a dream can be considered a similar secondary function of dreaming.

It is hard to be certain that remembering the dream is essential. Did our hunter-gatherer ancestors remember dreams and think about them much? We don't know. But I suggest that the weaving-into-memory function took place whether or not they remembered, and perhaps the new connections manifested themselves later when a similar problem or similar emotional concern arose. And in the women who dreamt of "Jim" turning into Father, we can wonder whether this dream might have been useful even if they had not woken up and made the connection in waking. The new connection might have allowed new possibilities of action, even without the intervening step of remembering a dream and saying, "Aha, Jim is so much like my father. I wonder if this relationship is right for me."

Quite possibly, the memory systems can become reconnected and reintegrated without our ever having to think about the dream while awake, but there's no way to be certain. Elias Howe, while trying to devise a sewing machine, had a famous dream which involved African natives dancing around him with spears. He noticed that each spear had a hole through its tip and he says that this provided the final link, which allowed him to design a sewing machine with a hole through the tip of the needle. Perhaps Howe's mind was already making the necessary connections and he would have solved his design problem at some point without remembering this specific dream, but the dream certainly brought the process into focus, or perhaps sped it up.

It is fairly rare that a dream makes a connection that leads to an insight as dramatically as in the cases of Howe or Kekule (who reported that a dream of snakes catching their tails in their mouths led him to discover the ring structure of the benzene molecule) (for details of these and many other discoveries in dreams see Barrett 2001). Often the connections coming up in the dream do not make any obvious sense (as seen by our focused waking minds). Still, they are our own connections, and our own memory reintegrations, guided by our own emotions. Remembering the dream and thinking about it can give us an additional chance to work on the material. Things are being put together in a new way, which may or may not be immediately obvious and useful, but in my view it is worth keeping track of one's dreams and going back to them once in a while even if they originally seem confused or almost random. One can, at times, find something useful in the dreams later on or by looking at a whole series of dreams rather than a single one.

FUNCTIONS OF DREAMING: CONCLUSIONS

We have discussed a number of ways in which making connections can be adaptive and useful. I think the most basic function of dreaming consists of connecting new material with old material in memory systems, reorganizing the memory systems, guided by emotion. This is not a consolidation of memory, but a weaving-in, an integration of memory systems. I believe this is going on all the time in dreaming whether or not we remember the dreams and pay attention to them. The connections are made or broadened, and the next time a similar situation arises, new associations and patterns will be available, I believe this happens even if the connections are not noticed and thought about in the waking state. However, when we do remember dreams and are able to think about them, we might as well examine them and maybe learn something about ourselves, or about a problem we've been struggling with, in a more direct manner. This can be considered a secondary function of dreaming.

Some years ago I wrote a paper called "Making connections in a safe place: Is dreaming psychotherapy?" (Hartmann 1995). This paper considered many similarities between dreaming and the process of psychodynamic psychotherapy. Many of these similarities can be summarized in the phrase "making connections in a safe place." The main process in both cases is making connections, guided of course by emotion. The "safe place" in dreaming consists of lying in bed combined with the muscular inhibition of REM sleep, so that we are not running around acting out our emotions and concerns—which could be dangerous—but lying quietly in bed and dreaming them. In therapy, the "safe place" consists not only of a quiet soundproof room, but also of the alliance—the gradually developing trust in the therapist, which allows the work of therapy to take place. To make the place "safe," the therapist must be absolutely reliable, working for the benefit of the patient, and not allowing his or her own needs to interfere.

Obviously there are many differences as well, but the similarities discussed suggest the possibility that the basic functions of dreaming may be similar to the functions of therapy. In both situations, emotionally important material arises, is examined, reorganized, and reconnected. This refers of course to the primary function of dreaming, discussed above, which occurs whether or not the dream is later remembered and thought about. When the dream is remembered, the secondary functions enter in, and one can then make use of the dream in other ways, including discussing the dream with a psychotherapist if one happens to be in therapy.

Although it is not easy to prove, I think it likely that dreaming has functions along the lines summarized above. And since dreaming is a form of cortical activation occurring most easily and most often in REM sleep, we can consider our conclusions to apply as well to the functions of REM sleep at the cortical level.

12 The Functions of the Continuum

Considering dreaming as one end of the focused-waking-to-dreaming continuum can clarify the question of function. Aside from a specific function for the dreaming end (see last chapter), it seems obvious that the entire continuum has an adaptive function. It is useful for us to be able to think in a focused manner at times and at other times to daydream or to dream. The broad, loose connections of dreaming can provide a different perspective and can help us make important decisions and discoveries.

The sixth and last point of the contemporary theory—that the entire continuum has a function—is very difficult to prove or even to approach experimentally, but it appears to me to need no proof. It seems self-evident. As we think of human beings living normal human lives (now or in ancestral times), focused-waking-thought is obviously useful. It is clearly important and functional for us to be able to think directly and clearly, to accomplish a task, to make and to carry out plans for the future. When we are in the outfield trying to catch a fly ball, we turn our minds/brains insofar as possible into navigational machines to observe and calculate the ball's trajectory, and move in exactly the right way to meet it. We try not to let our emotional concerns or our daydreams influence us while we are engaged in this pursuit. There may be stunningly beautiful cloud formations above us or a distant storm approaching. A close friend may be in the hospital. But, it is important for us to maintain our narrow focus and not be distracted. We do not want to think broadly or loosely. Similarly, when we are balancing a checkbook or doing some kind of math problem, we want to focus directly and totally on the task for a time, with as little distraction as possible.

However, focused waking thought is not what we need all the time. It sometimes gets us into a channel or a rut. We miss the obvious similarities between boyfriend and father. Our thinking is stuck and can't make the broad imaginative leaps sometimes required. This is where daydreaming and dreaming are useful. A large number of creative thinkers, in science as well as art, have emphasized the importance of daydreaming and fantasy in their creative work. Dreaming too has played a role in any number of new ideas in the arts and sciences (for a review see Barrett 2001). In some of the most famous cases, such as Kekule's (mentioned above), there is a great deal of debate as to whether the crucial insight occurred in a dream, during sleep, or rather in a waking fantasy or daydream (Strunz 1993). This is an important question if one thinks of dreams as meteorites from an alien world (see Chapter 9) but unimportant when one thinks in terms of the continuum.

It's not just a matter of new discoveries. The broad connections of dreaming can be useful in helping to make major life decisions such as choosing one's direction or path in life. It is striking that we in the modern Western world make no such systematic use of our dreams, while most other cultures have found a place for dreams in their organization of life.

As an important example, let's consider a life decision faced by young people all over the world. "What is my place in the world? What course shall I take?" (Sometimes abbreviated inadequately "career choice"). We often expect young people to explore a few possibilities, study, try a few jobs, and see what appeals to them. For most of us in the West there is no institutional method for making such a choice. We should be aware, however, that some cultures have established a methodology for career choice, and often dreams play a prominent role in it.

In a number of indigenous North and South American societies, a young man – in some cases a young woman too – is traditionally sent out on a "dream quest" at some time around puberty. The aim is for the young person to go off alone and (in some settings with the aid of food deprivation, sleep deprivation, or mild hallucinogens) to experience an important dream, which will show him a future path. It may also show him a guide or guardian spirit to help him. The dream – either directly in its manifest content, or with the help of interpretation after the youth's return – will help him decide on a career: whether to become a warrior, a farmer, or perhaps a shaman.

Here is one example I have mentioned previously (Hartmann 1998/2001). Irving Hallowell, a well-known anthropologist who worked with the Ojibwa, who lives in what is now Ontario and Manitoba, reports (1966):

> Dream fasts generally served as initiation rituals for Ojibwa boys (although there are accounts of Ojibwa girls going on dream fasts

> as well). Before leaving for the fast, the boy was given carefully washed clothes and a specially dyed animal skin to sleep on. He would then head into the forest with his father, grandfather, or other male relatives, who would help the boy find a suitable spot to build a wasizon (a sleeping platform up in the trees). The boy would spend up to ten days and nights on the wasizon, alone and fasting, until he had a dream in which a pawagan (spirit being or other-than-human being) bestowed a blessing on him.

One particular boy's dream experience was described to Hallowell as follows:

> *When I was a boy I went out to an island to fast. My father paddled me there. For several nights I dreamt of an ogima (chief or superior person). Finally he said to me, "Grandson, I think you are now ready to go with me." Then ogima began dancing around me as I sat there on a rock and when I happened to glance down at my body I noticed that I had grown feathers. Soon I felt just like a bird, a golden eagle. Ogima had turned into an eagle also and off he flew towards the South. I spread my wings and flew after him in the same direction. After a while we arrived at a place where there were lots of tents and lots of people. It was the home of the Summer Birds.*

Hallowell adds that, "…after returning North again the boy was left at their starting point after his guardian spirit had promised help whenever he wanted it. The boy's father came for him and took him home again." We are not told about the course of the boy's life, except that for the Ojibwa the eagle suggests a leadership role.

Is this widespread practice simply an irrational superstition? I think not. I believe we can understand it as an attempt by these various cultures to make use of the connecting powers of dreaming to put together previously unconnected themes in the young person's life. Obviously, the issue of choosing a path for life is an emotionally important problem for the young person. Furthermore, the preparations for the dream, sometimes including days of fasting and contemplating one's future and sometimes months of instruction by tribal elders as to the "career opportunities" open to a young person, etc., make certain that the issue becomes an especially powerful emotional concern at the time of the dream. In this situation — not dissimilar from the situations after trauma and stress, which we have discussed before — the dreaming mind will take the emotionally meaningful concern and make connections with any related material within the memory nets. And the dream may very well come up with an important connection in the form of a Central Image — a metaphoric picture based on the youth's wishes, fears, other emotional concerns, and his abilities and past experiences.

In fact, I know some modern Westerners who have made use of their dreams in this way even though it is not legitimized by our culture. They tried making a career choice by thinking carefully about possibilities, making lists of the pros and cons of various options, and so on. They told me that this sort of thinking and list-making may have helped a bit, but was not satisfactory. They felt good about the decision only after they had a dream about it. And again it does not have to be a night dream. Some have spoken of a "vision," such as, "I saw my whole future life spread out before me, in vivid color. I was a lawyer practicing in a small town and the whole thing just seemed wrong. I had better rethink my career."

Consistent with this view, a series of recent studies investigated lay peoples' interpretations of their own dreams using a total of 1,137 participants from a number of Eastern and Western cultures. The results showed that overall most people do pay attention to their dreams in one way or another and make use of their dreams in their everyday lives (Morewedge and Norton 2009).

People who are poor dream re-callers can sometimes use fantasies and daydreams to help with important decisions. Alcohol and various drugs have been used for similar purposes. According to Herodotus, the ancient Persian kings famously refused to take a major action such as starting a war unless they had decided to do it while sober, and then had agreed on the same decision when drunk. This is not exactly the use of dreams or daydreams we have been discussing, but we can understand it in the same way. In making an important decision, we should not rely totally on a single, sober focused-waking-thought frame of mind, but attempt to look at the same problem from another perspective. Something like this Persian custom could at times be helpful to us. I am not suggesting the use of alcohol, but rather allowing ourselves to consider the decision from various points along our focused-waking-to-dreaming continuum.

I have no doubt that it is useful to us to have the full range of mental functioning available, and that having this entire range available was adaptive in the phylogenetic development of the species. The entire continuum, including the emotion-guided memory-integration aspects of dreaming, can be useful even if we do not consciously remember dreams and make directed use of them. But when we do remember dreams, why not help the process along and make further waking use of the connections and associations provided by our dreams?

What I am saying is that it is obviously adaptive to our species to have available the entire continuum of mental functioning. There are many times when clear, precise focused thought is essential. But there are other times when our focused thinking is stuck. We are in a rut. We cannot see the obvious similarities between Jim and Father. We cannot quite decide what we want to do with our lives. We are not sure that this relationship is right for us. We cannot seem to make the final imaginative leap we need to solve the problem or create the new work. This is when we are fortunate in having available the rest of the continuum, enabling us to think more freely, and associate more broadly—in other words, enabling us to daydream and to dream.

13 Implications for Understanding and Making Use of Dreams: Alone, in a Group, or in Therapy

Dreams are an important part of us and they can help us understand others and ourselves. But they are part us, part of our mental functioning. They are not alien intrusions. They are not written in a foreign language that needs to be translated word for word. Dreams are where we make the broadest imaginative leaps. Dreams can help in understanding, discovering, creating. They can also be appreciated as works of art or almost-art. Dreams do not have a single "translation" or meaning. They need not be and indeed cannot be completely explained or understood.

I hope that our previous discussion makes it clear that I believe dreaming has a primary function in making connections and integration of memory—functions which occur whether or not a dream is remembered in the morning. However, when we do remember a dream it can be useful to us in other ways, which we discussed under possible secondary functions of dreaming, including self-knowledge, which can be life altering, and making new scientific or artistic discoveries. I have little doubt, based on many years of experience, that working with dreams can be helpful in self-knowledge and self-awareness. Numerous others have made the same discovery.

Dream interpretation played a prominent part in Freudian psychoanalysis for many years, though it has been somewhat deemphasized recently. It is still a very prominent part of Jungian analysis. The various schools of dynamic psychotherapy have always paid lip service to the importance of dreams, though in actual practice the time constraints of the usual once-a-week therapy have tended to make serious work with dreams impractical.

Outside of formal psychoanalysis and psychotherapy there is a popular movement, sometimes called dream-working, in which people get together in pairs or small groups to discuss and try to understand their dreams with or without a leader or a formal agenda (Hillman 1990). Often these informal dream groups, which appear to be very helpful to the participants, function more or less within guidelines suggested by Montague Ullman in several publications (1988, 2006). I personally know a great many people, both professionals and nonprofessionals, who are taking part in such informal dream groups, and in fact I have been part of one group myself for almost twenty years. In such groups there is no therapeutic goal, but only a general interest in dreams and a desire to get to know oneself better by looking at one's dreams. Most participants seem to appreciate and benefit from such groups. The clearest benefit is in allowing a number of minds to think about and make suggestions about a given dream and thus help the dreamer to see more than she or he can see alone. This seems to work regardless of the theoretical orientation, if any, of the group. In my experience the groups often open up the dream, bring up interesting new possibilities for the dreamer to think about, but they seldom come up with a single complete "interpretation" of a dream.

HOW DREAMS ARE INTERPRETED

The Contemporary Theory of Dreaming has important implications for the use of dreams in and out of psychotherapy. Before discussing these implications, let me review briefly the major ways dreams are currently worked on or "interpreted" in therapy and in ongoing dream groups. First is the technique Freud called free association, which depends on the use of chains of association. The patient or dreamer first relates the dream in as much detail as possible. He or she is then asked to consider each element of the dream in turn and say exactly what comes to mind—what associations arise, and then to continue associating freely to the new material that comes up. In this way a number of sometimes lengthy chains of association are formed, which often converge on certain problems or concerns in the person's mind. These points of convergence, or nodal points, often form a group of thoughts which are considered to be the "latent" dream—the thoughts that underlie the "manifest dream." In Freud's view, these latent thoughts always take the form of one or more wishes. Hence, his view that when a dream is truly understood it turns out to be the fulfillment of a wish.

Jungian psychoanalysts work with dreams somewhat differently. They usually choose one piece of the dream which seems especially important to the dreamer or the analyst and then try to "amplify" that element of the dream. Amplification can involve association, developing further related imagery and feeling, and discussing stories or myths which involve that same element. This often uncovers important material which was previously unconscious for the dreamer. In addition to amplification, the dreamer may also be asked to use "active imagination," which means starting with a dream element and imagining a new story about it.

The techniques known as Gestalt dream interpretation (Perls, Heffeline and Goodman 1951) involve the dreamer play-acting each character in the dream, sometimes even each animal or object in the dream and examining what this object might feel like, do, or think. Again, change of viewpoint often leads to important knowledge for the dreamer. There are also techniques involving experiencing the dream in one's body and techniques involving painting or artwork, dancing or singing—all ways of re-experiencing the dreams in an attempt to expand our understanding (Ellis 1988; Craig 1990; Zwig 1990).

Ullman's technique (1988, 2006) of group dream work involves relating the dream to a group of people in a safe setting and letting each member of the group ask questions and provide his or her own associations to the dream or thoughts about the dream. The basic idea is that multiple minds are better than one and that someone else may see something significant in the dream which the dreamer himself has missed. It is important that the group members do not try to convince the dreamer about what they think the dream means. They are encouraged to make suggestions along the lines of "if it were my dream, I would consider…" It is up to the dreamer to decide what suggestions to use.

In my experience, all these very different techniques can be helpful and all of them can lead to the uncovering of new themes or thoughts of which the dreamer was previously unaware. All the techniques can be useful, but they can sometimes be misused. In general, whatever technique is being used, it is best to let the dreamer have the last word. Any thoughts or interpretations suggested by a therapist or group member should only be considered possibilities or hypotheses. A useful insight or "interpretation" must be made by the dreamer or at least feel completely right to the dreamer. A marvelous interpretation that makes perfect sense to the analyst or therapist but not to the dreamer is useless. It is up to the dreamer to decide what is useful or what seems true. I actually prefer the idea of "useful" to "true" because even the dreamer may not be always be right and the dreamer is capable of self-deception as we will see in an example below.

In addition to these more or less formal techniques, people informally make use of their own dreams in many ways and have been doing so for millennia. Most of us can get useful information or insights from our dreams without officially "interpreting" them. And some of us actually make new discoveries based on our dreams (Barrett 2001).

MAKING USE OF THE ENTIRE CONTINUUM

As I mentioned, the Contemporary Theory of Dreaming has some major implications for working with one's dreams or dream interpretation. First of all, I would like to convince even my hardheaded scientist friends that being aware of one's dreams and examining them can often be useful. I suggest that we may as well make use of the entire continuum. Why not let our minds help us in whatever part of the continuum they happen to be functioning? Why neglect the entire daydreaming/dreaming end of the continuum? I believe that never examining one's dreams is depriving us of a potentially important aspect of ourselves.

Some of the hardheaded types claim that dreams are just too illogical or bizarre to be worth our attention. Personally, I find such a view bizarre! (But perhaps I should simply say that these scientists are functioning in a very thick boundary mode). Their view implies that we should attend only to our most logical, straightforward linear thoughts and discard the rest. Following this line of reasoning would mean paying no attention to the arts, either. Art is seldom linear and logical, it has no immediate use, and new art is often called illogical, far-out, or bizarre. This view would deprive us of some of the most intriguing, creative portions of ourselves. I also believe that such a view belittles art, considering it as purely decoration or entertainment, rather than an integral part of our world.

I am certainly not arguing that we should use only our dreaming minds or that we should substitute our dream ideas for our waking ideas. (That would truly be bizarre!) I believe we can obtain new insights or ideas in dreams but we must of course wake up and check out these ideas in our very different focused waking mode of functioning. Why not make use of everything we have?

WHERE TO START WORKING ON THE DREAM

Getting down to actual work with dreams, by therapists or others, our theory may be useful in dealing with a practical issue—where to start working on a dream, where to "get into" the dream. In Freudian analysis this question is bypassed since associations are sought to every element of the dream. Unfortunately, time does not usually allow for complete Freudian free association. In current practice, where a patient is seen once per week or less, it seems impossible to even try to understand a dream. No matter how psychodynamic the therapist or how interested in dreams, there is just no time. Many therapists have told me that they usually don't do any serious work with dreams since there's so much important stuff going on, so many current problems, etc. Besides, they tell me, "I just don't know where to start."

I would suggest, based on our discussion in the last chapters, that when time is limited, as it almost always is in therapy, a good place to start is with the Central Image of the dream. This usually leads quickly to important underlying emotions. This is a good starting point, but of course not an ending point. Becoming aware of underlying emotions is often only the beginning of understanding, but it is important and can quickly lead into significant new material, even when time is limited. Interestingly, two Jungian analysts who heard me lecture on the Central Image, told me later that when they are choosing a part of a patient's dream to "amplify" they almost always choose what I call the Central Image, though they had not previously used that term. Of course this is only a general suggestion—every clinical situation is different and there may be times when it could be dangerous to start with the Central Image and get to important emotional material immediately. In such a situation the therapist might choose to start with more peripheral parts of the dream.

THE IMPORTANCE OF EMOTION

Next, we can make use of the theory's emphasis on the importance of the emotion underlying each dream. Even a quick attempt to identify, examine, and sometimes intensify the underlying emotion can be useful. My associate Robert Kunzendorf has been using intensification of emotion in a research project with volunteer subjects who want to discuss their dreams (Kunzendorf 2007). The person is asked 1) to write down a dream, 2) write down an initial interpretation of the dream, and 3) write down a reinterpretation of the dream after identifying the "underlying emotion or major emotional concern," and spending five minutes feeling the emotion and gradually intensifying it, noticing any thought or imagery that comes to mind.

This was research and not meant as therapy. Yet here are the results in one woman. The dream:

> *I am asleep but I think I am awake. The room is perfectly detailed as though I were awake and looking. A man comes out of my closet. I am*

> *terrified beyond description. I feel desperate to escape but I cannot move. I feel a deadly weight on my chest. I want to scream but cannot. I realize I am having a nightmare and if I can move or make a sound I will wake up. I struggle to move just a toe. The man presents a terror to me worse than death. I try again and again to scream "No." The word comes out in grunts until I finally wake up screaming.*

She mentions that this is a recurring dream that first occurred twenty years previously and last occurred seven days before the present session. Her initial interpretation:

> *I believe this dream, nightmare — which is reoccurring, is my mind's way of dealing with a childhood trauma that I can't completely remember. It baffles me because it seems it would be easier for me to remember the trauma than to go through the torment of this nightmare year after year.*

Then she identified the feeling as *terror* and tried to intensify and clarify for five minutes. She then wrote a reinterpretation of her dream:

> *The emotion is an unholy white terror. It is fear that goes beyond the fear of death. It is a fear of eternal suffering. The man in the dream was my stepfather. What he wanted from me was sex. Yet to my child mind in the darkness of night, I felt he wanted to kill me but more than kill me. It felt as though he would own my soul and my self for all eternity. Imagine how it would feel for someone you despised to own every part of your body and mind.*

This was not a patient in psychotherapy. However, it illustrates how clarifying and intensifying an emotion underlying the dream, even in just five minutes, can sometimes lead to significant new insights. In this case it apparently led to a new and altered memory of important childhood events.

A DREAM CANNOT BE COMPLETELY TRANSLATED. GETTING THE "GIST" OF THE DREAM.

A related point is that even if you are very interested in dreams, you need not interpret every single one of your dreams in detail. Life just is not long enough, so in general I would recommend working on those of your dreams that seem special or fascinating or important to you for whatever reason.

More important, a major implication of the view we have been developing is that usually no complete "translation" is possible. The dream is there, as part of our mental functioning, but it is not neatly translatable into our waking thoughts or waking language. The "latent dream thoughts" (Freud) do not represent a complete understanding or translation of the dream. I cannot agree with Freud's view of the dream as only a "manifest dream" which can be completely translated into a group of underlying thoughts (the "latent dream"). We can indeed work on a dream and free associate to the elements in the dream. Underlying thoughts and especially underlying emotional concerns usually emerge. Discussion of the underlying "latent" thoughts can definitely contribute to our understanding, but in my view we can no more substitute the latent thoughts for the dream than we can substitute a critic's explanation of a work of art for the work of art itself.

I suggest that probably all we can usefully do is get to the "gist" of the dream. Getting the "gist" involves appreciating the dream as a whole, looking at the connections to see if there is anything new or surprising, and certainly examining the Central Image, to help identify the underlying emotion and concerns. Most often that is all we can do with certainty, in terms of understanding the dream, and perhaps it is all we should do.

Of course it is possible to go further, much further if we wish, but now we are analyzing the patient—the person—not interpreting the dream. Freud spent forty-three pages analyzing the first dream in his book "The Interpretation of Dreams" (1953 [1900]), called "The Dream of Irma's Injection." Others have devoted hundreds of pages to adding more interpretation of this same dream. And indeed many of the interpretations seem very plausible, though there is always a danger that we will be analyzing our own projections rather than the patient's dream. But even if this danger is avoided and the analyst is very careful to stick with the dream and dutifully obtain the patient's associations to each element as Freud suggests, we frequently find that the one dream can be examined interminably. Its associations do not produce a few simple intersecting lines of association; rather, they lead outward to involve almost everything in the patient's life. Morton Reiser, for instance, has illustrated in detail the multiple lines and loops of association that can come from a single dream (1990, 1997). Maybe there is no problem with this. After all, everything in the mind is connected and all the many lines of association can help in our understanding.

However, I want to emphasize again that we are now analyzing the whole patient, not a specific dream. In terms of understanding a given dream, we have gone too far. What I mean by "too far" is this: when we spend weeks obtaining associations to a patient's dream, or to our own dream, and keep careful track of all the associated material, we soon find that the associative chains include recent material—events that happened after the date of the dream—and often this material fits into the chain of association just as well as the older material, even though it could not have played a role in producing the dream. Thus, I cannot agree with Freud that tracing these lines of association will show us exactly what produced the dream. We are now analyzing the entire patient, or our entire selves, taking a dream as a starting point. If useful material emerges, why not go on, but we are no longer interpreting a particular dream. From a clinical viewpoint this is fine, assuming there is enough time and interest; however, we cannot claim that we are simply following the chains of association that will lead us to a complete understanding of the genesis and meaning of this particular dream. And, as mentioned, I think we are usually fooling ourselves if we seek and find a complete understanding (translation) of a dream.

I have said above that the dream is not written in a foreign language that needs to be translated word for word. But of course we can speak metaphorically of a "language of dreams." I would say that insofar as there is a language of dreaming, it is connection, cross-connection, metaphor as we have discussed. It is the language of creation, of poetry, of art. Instead of insisting on "translating" every bit of a dream, I suggest that we generally should be satisfied with the "gist" of the dream, which is all we can really do in terms of interpretation.

But we need not stop there. When we have a truly impressive dream, a "big" dream, it can be so striking that it calls out for attention, though not necessarily "interpretation." In fact, interpretation may be the wrong approach. Interpretation emphasizes finding a meaning, a "latent dream" underlying the dream, and then more or less substituting that for the dream. Of course dreaming is meaningful, as is thought, fantasy, daydreaming, and artistic creation. But there is not a single meaning to be "extracted." I suggest that rather than translating, we can accept, we can appreciate, we can admire, we can learn.

It is possible to admire or appreciate the dream—especially a "big" dream—the way we appreciate a work of art. Dreaming is produced at the loose/creative end of our continuum. Why not consider it as a kind of work of art or at least the beginning of a work of art? Is this a surprising idea? A work of art, like a dream, involves a recombination of old material in a new way, guided by emotion. Isn't a new work of art often described as "grabbing our emotions" and even as "dream-like?" And when it first appears, it is often called "bizarre!"

The American "can-do" attitude is, "if you're doing something, do it well, do it perfectly." In this sense we feel we have to "totally understand this dream." I do not recommend that attitude, though a lot of people will be disappointed if they cannot do a thing perfectly or completely. Personally, I do not think we ever totally understand a dream.

A DREAM CANNOT BE COMPLETELY UNDERSTOOD, BUT A DREAM CAN CHANGE YOUR LIFE.

Dreams can be a hint, a gist, a painting, a poem. You should not expect to understand the dream completely. But that does not mean that dreams have no effect on your life. The effects can be dramatic even if the dream only gives you a hint or a possibility, a new connection or association that you hadn't been aware of. "Wow, Jim really is so much like my Father, odd that I hadn't noticed. Is there a lot of related stuff I haven't been aware of? Am I being pulled somewhere I don't want to go?" The hint can be emotional, like noticing an emotion you hadn't been aware of or can involve a person, or an area in your life. "Hmmm, if that comes up so strongly in my dreams, it must be more important than I thought."

Even the very common dreams we have spoken of can lead to changes. For instance, consider the common dream of being in a car going downhill and the brakes not working, dreamt by someone worried about a relationship. There is no translating homunculus in the head saying, "Let's see now, how shall I picture this relationship? I'll use the metaphor (symbol) of a car in motion—that usually works pretty well. And I'll symbolize my fear of the relationship getting out of control by a car whose brakes don't work. And I'll use a hill—the car going down hill to picture the danger—to suggest that maybe things are going downhill in this relationship." No, it happens all at once: the emotion of anxiety and concern about the relationship pulls together material in the memory stores that is related to this theme. The car image is likely to be available anyway; maybe there is a specific car that gets in because of a connection with someone else who recently had an accident, or who recently ended a relationship. Many different images may come up in connection with the relationship, but the emotion of worry makes it more likely that some will be chosen rather than others. Becoming more aware of this emotion or concern and examining it can be very important. It allows you to think over the relationship in your waking life and consider making changes.

Sometimes a powerful dream can make a very dramatic change and even save your life. A friend and colleague of mine, William Dement, a well-known sleep researcher, used to be a heavy smoker. Many years ago he had a dream with a powerful Central Image in which he saw an x-ray of his lungs, which showed advanced lung cancer (Dement and Vaughan 1999). In the dream, he discussed this condition with doctors and family and realized sadly that there was no hope for recovery. He woke up with a terrified, poignant feeling that he would never live to see his young children grow up. He then realized that this was after all a dream rather than reality and that he might be able to change things. Indeed, he immediately stopped smoking and has never gone back to the habit in the last forty years. He is still alive at the age of eighty.

Here is another example of a powerful dream that had long-lasting effects. Kathleen Sullivan, who now runs several talk shows on dreams, reported a dream that apparently changed her life (Sullivan 1998). At the time of the dream she was a teacher. She dreamt of taking her class on a fieldtrip in the woods. One of the students called to her to see an enormous spider web, perhaps eighteen feet in diameter, with a great eagle splayed out—caught in the web. She says she felt a grief and horror that she had never before experienced. She fell to her knees sobbing hysterically and awakened with a feeling of great anguish. She says that the need to understand this dream became the focus of her life, and it soon led her to abandon teaching and adopt her present career. I have heard only a few dramatic medical examples such as Dement's, but I've heard of many dreams such as Sullivan's, which resulted in important life changes.

In some of these dramatic examples, the dream's Central Image grabs our attention, much as does a work of art when it really "gets to us." Rilke, in a famous sonnet, admires a powerful "glowing torso" of Apollo, which he describes in emotional crescendo for thirteen and a half lines and then ends: "… *du must dein leben endern*" ("you must change your life!").

Of course, the Ojibwa boy in the last chapter and thousands of others in many different cultures have also used dreams to change or determine the course of their lives. On a less dramatic level, awareness of our emotion lets us make changes. A very typical dream pictures a feeling of anxiety related to not being quite on top of things, not being as prepared as others. These concerns are easily pictured in the common dream themes: "I'm not properly dressed," "I'm naked or half-naked while others are dressed properly," or "I can't find the exam room I'm assigned to." This is a very common emotion or group of emotions, and it appears to produce this very common anxiety dream. But often the dream occurs in a dreamer who is avoiding these feelings, pretending that everything's fine, nothing is bothering her or him. Simply becoming aware of the anxiety and relating it to underlying problems can lead to making changes in one's life.

The Contemporary Theory suggests that we may understand the "gist" of a dream, and perhaps make use of this, but we will not be able to completely understand or explain a given dream. At best, if we know a lot about the dreamer's emotions and concerns we can make some limited predictions. If we know the dreamer is greatly aroused emotionally, we can predict that the dreams will have especially powerful imagery. And if we know that one emotion (terror, sadness, guilt, etc.) is dominant, we can make some guess as to the sort of images that will likely occur in a series of dreams. We can predict statistically, as in the 9/11 study, but we cannot predict the content of an individual dream any more than we can predict perfectly the content of a reverie or a daydream.

USEFUL INTERPRETATIONS, NOT "TRUE" INTERPRETATIONS. BEWARE OF A "TRUE INTERPRETATION."

I'm not proposing a single technique of dream interpretation that would be useful in every dream. Freudian free association can be very helpful, as can Jungian amplification and Gestalt role-playing. For some people, acting, dancing, or playing with the dream in some way can produce new insight. Why not? If a dream seems powerful or important, by all means stick with it, work on it, play with it. The Contemporary Theory does not suggest that one technique is always best. Do whatever feels right to you.

As discussed above, the Contemporary Theory does make a few suggestions, as to where to start and when to stop. Especially if you're involved in psychotherapy and time is limited. If you want to quickly get to something emotionally important, I'd suggest starting with the most powerful image, the Central Image, or start with whatever feels most powerful. I am not suggesting absolute rules; there is no absolute measure. In clinical workshops I've called the CI "the fast lane on the royal road to the unconscious." And as mentioned, Jungians have indeed told me that when they choose a part of the dream to "amplify," it is very often the CI.

As to the question of when to stop: don't expect a complete "aha experience," a complete understanding. Stop whenever you want to with the understanding that you can revisit the dream later. Some keep returning to a dream for their entire lives. Be satisfied with a hint, a tentative answer; don't expect complete enlightenment.

In other words, some of my overall suggestions would be to start with the CI; get the "gist" of the dream; examine the new connections and the underlying emotion. You may want to stop there. Or, possibly look at other dreams to get a pattern. Stop there if your interest is in that specific dream. If you are analyzing or understanding a whole person, who could be you, then by all means, go on. But you should realize that you are no longer trying to understand a specific dream, but rather the whole person. Finally, if you have a big, beautiful dream, by all means admire it; treat it as a work of art.

I am sorry if I am disappointing people. I know some who desperately crave clear answers from their dreams. Some crave spiritual enlightenment the way others crave religious certainty. Personally, I am a bit of a skeptic. In many areas I do not believe in absolute certainty or absolute truth. Learn from the dream, yes, but don't be too sure. Some crave the truth from an expert or guru. Many will say, "Well, I realize I shouldn't just accept some expert's or guru's interpretation. If it's my dream, the interpretation is true if it feels right to me." I agree, but only in part. Don't take someone else's word for the meaning of your dream. But, surprisingly, I'd go further: even if it does feel right to the dreamer, even if both the dreamer and the therapist or expert agree on the meaning of a dream, that still does not guarantee its truth.

I remember back in the 1960s working on a patient's dreams with a group of other young doctors in training. The patient was a young gay man who had a dream about a large, powerful dangerous woman who clearly represented his mother. The senior psychiatrist/psychoanalyst who was teaching us said that this was a very obvious dream that provided clear insight about how this young man's mother had caused him to become homosexual. (This was an accepted view of the origins of homosexuality at the time.) The interpretation made sense to all the doctors present. And, interestingly, this interpretation was discussed with the patient who also agreed completely!

Looking back on it now, I would say that most probably the doctors were wrong and the patient was likewise wrong. We, and our teacher, were under the influence of more or less dominant social theories. So I would argue that even when everyone agrees, including the dreamer, we do not necessarily have the truth—certainly not absolute truth. I hope you, dear reader, will not go away with the message that yes, we were really ignorant forty years ago; we know much better now. Rather, the message should be that we are still ignorant now, about many things, in ways we probably don't recognize right now, but perhaps will in forty years. Let's be careful. In interpreting dreams, let's be satisfied with new connections and new insights that might give us a broader view or perhaps make a change in our lives. Let's not expect total truth.

There is another sense in which we need a little humility. Even if our current theory turns out to be entirely correct it does not allow us to predict what a particular person will dream about on a particular night (nor of course does any other theory of dreaming). Even in what I have called the simplest case, someone who has just experienced a major trauma, I cannot claim that all the dreams will be tidal wave dreams. I've shown that tidal wave dreams are more probable in this situation, and that more powerful images are found (quantifiably), but I can't predict the exact image. This should not be surprising. We don't expect that every waking thought or reverie of this traumatized person will involve the trauma either. Overall we are very far from being able to predict any form of mental content with certainty.

THE "BIG" DREAM: AWE, WONDER, AND MYSTERY

Most people who recall a lot of dreams occasionally experience a "big" dream, such as in the examples above. Freud and Jung each discussed one powerful dream that stayed with them for their entire lives. Freud speaks of his dream, which he says occurred in his seventh or eighth year, "It was a very vivid dream and in it I saw my beloved mother, with a peculiarly peaceful, sleeping expression on her features, being carried into the room by two (or three) people with birds' beaks, and laid upon the bed" (Freud 1953 [1900], 583). Jung's dream that he originally had in early childhood involves him going down a series of stairs into a basement where he sees "a huge phallic pillar on a magnificent throne" and is told that it is "the man-eater" (Jung 1965, 12).

The term "big dream" has been used widely, but not clearly defined. In a recent paper (Hartmann 2008a), I tried to examine "big" dreams by subdividing them into four categories more amenable to study: memorable dreams (remembered a long time), important dreams (identified as important by the dreamer), significant dreams (so identified by the dreamer), and a group of "impactful" dreams (impactful in the sense that they led to a scientific or artistic achievement). In all four groups of dreams, the CI intensity was very high—much higher than in available control groups of dreams. This is also consistent with my impression from numerous informal interviews: when I asked friends and colleagues to tell me their most memorable dream, or their most important dream, they almost invariably told a dream with a powerful CI. My conclusion was that it is the powerful CI that makes a "big" dream "big."

I have not yet done a formal comparison of "emotions pictured" (see Figure 3.1 and Chapter 3) in the dreams from these various studies, but I was struck by one fact. Overall, we tend to have a lot of "negative" emotions such as anxiety pictured in our dreams, and indeed in our many dream series and studies the first three emotions (fear/terror, helplessness/vulnerability, and anxiety) are the emotions scored the most frequently as "emotions pictured" by the CIs. However, one of the "positive" emotions, called "awe/wonder/mystery," was scored surprisingly often. And this emotion or group of emotions was scored especially often in the "big" dreams, and in dreams of people with thin boundaries (see Chapter 10 and Hartmann 2008a).

Although awe/wonder/mystery, a group of emotions that could be called the spiritual emotions, are not usually listed among the basic human emotions, our data indicates that they are important in dreams, most especially in big or powerful dreams. At times the emotion is directly reported by the dreamer, but often no emotion is mentioned. The dreamer does not say "I was awe-struck" or "it was wondrous." The dream simply builds a powerful image (CI) which an observer or scorer decides may be picturing the emotions of awe / wonder / mystery. Such images and the emotions underlying them again lead us to what we experience with a great work of art or with an experience that feels spiritual. These emotions are certainly important in working with patients' dreams or our own dreams. And it is not surprising that dreaming, at the right end of the continuum, leads us readily to these essential human emotions.

THE DREAM AS ART. A DREAM-SCULPTURE.

As I've emphasized several times, a dream is part of us, not an alien intrusion. A dream lives at the outermost, loosest, least constrained, most creative end of the continuum of mental functioning. It's guided by emotion, so we should definitely pay attention to the emotion, whether directly felt in the dream, or pictured by the imagery (Central Image). And of course we can pay attention to any striking new connections. Sometimes that's all we can do. But then we can look at the dream, and once in a while feel "Wow, what a beautiful image!" or "Wow, what an intriguing idea!" or "Wow, I must change my life!" or just plain "Wow!" These are the same reactions we sometimes have to a powerful painting or poem or piece of music. And why not appreciate a dream the way we appreciate a work of art? They come from the same part of us.

For some, straightforward enjoyment is the way to appreciate art. That's fine. For others, the work of art becomes even more beautiful or impressive when it is put into some kind of context and discussed or analyzed. Fine again. Either way. So let it be with dreaming! Appreciate the dream as you appreciate art and don't expect absolute truth—don't expect to completely understand a big dream anymore than you expect to completely understand a great work of art.

At the focused-waking end of the continuum, tasks demand completion—we want the fly ball to fall "plunk" into our glove and that's it. We want to work at the math problem, figure out the answer, say "whew," and stop. But at the dreaming end of the continuum I don't believe that we need completion or that we can have completion. Is that frustrating? Or rather is that the beauty of it?

I had a big dream, an important-feeling dream some twenty years ago, that I have remembered ever since. It had a powerful Central Image: I was outdoors, showing people a large abstract sculpture. The sculpture was about eight feet tall, all glowing gold. It was beautiful. I was showing it to people, but it was not clear whether I had made it myself, or had found it there.

I've thought about that dream off and on. I don't quite understand it. But here's one association to the dream that came to me while writing this book:

> *After all my years of trying, I do not completely understand dreaming. I have tried to discover something important about the nature and the functions of dreaming. I've written a book about it. I'm showing my (big, glowing) ideas to people. But have I really discovered something? Or have I created something, invented something? Does it matter? Are the two processes—discovery and creation—really separable?*

References

Armor, D. 1973–4. Theta reliability and factor scaling. In H. Costner, (Ed.), *Sociological Methodology*. San Francisco: Jossey-Bass.

Aserinsky, E., and N. Kleitman. 1953. Regularly occurring periods of eye motility and concomitant phenomena during sleep. *Science* 118: 273–74.

Astic, L. and D. Jouvet-Mounier. 1971. Etude polygraphique et comportementale des etats de vigilance chez le Cobaye premature. *Physiology & Behavior* 7:59–64.

Barbuto, J., and B. Plummer. 1998. Mental boundaries as a new dimension of personality: a comparison of Hartmann's boundaries in the mind and Jung's psychological types. *Journal of Social Behavior and Personality* 13:421–436.

Barbuto, J. and B. Plummer. 2000. Mental boundaries and Jung's psychological types: a profile analysis. *Journal of Psychological Type* 54:17–21.

Barcaro, U., R. Calabrese, C. Cavallero, R. Diciotti, and C. Navona. 2002. Significance of automatically detected word recurrences in dream associations. *Dreaming* 12:93–107.

Barrett, D. 1979. The hypnotic dream: Its content in comparison to nocturnal dreams and waking fantasy. *Journal of Abnormal Psychology* 88: 584–591.

Barrett, D. 1989. The relationship of thin vs. thick boundaries to hypnotic susceptibility. Paper presented at the meetings of the Eastern Psychological Association. Boston, MA. April 1989.

Barrett, D. 1992. Just how lucid are lucid dreams? *Dreaming* 2:221–228.

Barrett, D. 1993. The "committee of sleep": A study of dream incubation for problem solving. *Dreaming* 3:115–122.

Barrett, D. 2001. *The Committee of Sleep*. New York: Crown Publishers.

Beal, S. 1989. The boundary characteristics of artists. (Unpublished doctoral dissertation, Boston University).

Beaulieu-Prévost, D., and A. Zadra. 2005. Dream recall frequency and attitude towards dreams: A reinterpretation of the relation. *Personality and Individual Differences* 38:919–927.

Belicki, K. 1992. Nightmare frequency versus nightmare distress: Relations to psychopathology and cognitive style. *Journal of Abnormal Psychology* 101:592–597.

Bell, M., R. Billington, and B. Becker. 1986. A scale for the assessment of object relations: reliability, validity, and factorial invariance. *Journal of Clinical Psychology* 42:733–741.

Bevis, J. 1986. Connectedness versus separateness: Understanding male/female differences in self and relationship. (Unpublished doctoral dissertation, Boston University).

Blagrove, M. and L. Akehurst. 2000. Personality and dream recall frequency: Further negative findings. *Dreaming* 10:139–148.

Blatt, S. J., and B.A. Ritzler. 1974. Thought disorder and boundary disturbances in psychosis. *Journal of Consulting and Clinical Psychology* 42:370–381.

Blatt, S. J., A. Besser, and R. Q. Ford. 2007. Two primary configurations of psychopathology and change in thought disorder in long-term intensive patient treatment of seriously disturbed young adults. *American Journal of Psychiatry* 164:1561–1567.

Bokert, E. 1967. The effects of thirst and a related verbal stimulus on dream reports. Doctoral dissertation, New York University (University Microfilm 68–6041, 1968).

Braun, A., T. Balkin, N. Wesenten, et al. 1997. Regional cerebral blood flow throughout the sleep-wake cycle. *Brain* 120:7.

Buckner, R. L., J. R. Andrews-Hanna, and D.L. Schacter. 2008. The brain's default network: Anatomy, function, and relevance to disease. In A. Kingstone and M. B. Miller (Eds.), *The Year of Cognitive Neuroscience 2008*. Malden, MA: Blackwell Publishing. pp. 1–38.

Cai, D. J., S. A. Mednick, E. M. Harrison, J. C. Kanady, and S. C. Mednick. 2009. REM, not incubation, improves creativity by priming associative networks. PNAS 106:10130–10134.

Cartwright, R. 1991. Dreams that work: The relation of dream incorporation to adaptation to stressful events. *Dreaming* 1:3–10.

Cartwright, R., and I. Romanek. 1978. Repetitive dreams of normal subjects. *Sleep Research* 7:174.

Cattell, R. B. 1966. The scree test for the number of factors. *Multivariate Behavioral Research* 1:245–276.

Cavallero, C., and P. Cicogna. 1993. Memory and dreaming. In C. Cavallero and D. Foulkes (Eds.), *Dreaming as Cognition*. New York: Harvester Wheatsheaf. pp. 38–57.

Cohen, D. B. 1974a. Toward a theory of dream recall. *Psychological Bulletin* 81:138–154.

Cohen, D. B. 1974b. Affective personality and presleep mood on dream recall. *Journal of Abnormal Psychology* 83:151–156.

Cohen, J. D., K. Dunbar, and J. L. McClelland. 1990. On the control of automatic processes: A parallel distributed processing account of the stroop effect. *Psychological Review* 97:332–361.

Coleridge, S. Cited in: W. Auden & L. Kronenberger, (Eds.), 1966. *The Viking Book ofAphorisms*. New York: Viking. p. 362.

Costa, P., and R. McCrae. 1992. Revised NEO Personality Inventory (NEO-PI-R) and NEO Five-Factor Inventory (NEO-FFI) Professional Manual. Odessa, FL: Psychological Assessment Resources.

Cowen, D. and R. Levin. 1995. The use of the Hartmann Boundary Questionnaire with an adolescent population. *Dreaming* 5:105–114.

Craig, P. E. 1990. An existential approach to dreamwork. In S. Krippner (Ed.), *Dreamtime & Dreamwork: Decoding the Language of the Night*. Los Angeles: Jeremy P. Tarcher, Inc. pp. 69–77.

Dement, W. and N. Kleitman. 1957. Cyclic variations in EEG during sleep and their relation to eye movements, body motility, and dreaming. *Electroencephology Clinical Neurophysiology* 9:673–690.

Dement, W., and C. Vaughan. 1999. *The Promise of Sleep*. New York: Delacorte.

Domhoff, W. G. 1996. *Finding Meaning in Dreams: A Quantitative Approach*. New York: Plenum.

Domhoff, W. G. 2003. *The Scientific Study of Dreams: Neural Networks, Cognitive Development, and Content Analysis*. Washington, DC: American Psychological Association.

Domhoff, W. G. 2007. Realistic simulation and bizarreness in dream content: past findings and suggestions for future research. In D. Barrett and P. McNamara (Eds.), *The New Science of Dreaming: Volume 2*. Westport, CT: Praeger. pp. 1–27.

Dorus, E., W. Dorus, and A. Rechtschaffen. 1971. The incidence of novelty in dreams. *Archives of General Psychiatry*, 25:364–368.

Earle, J. 1992. Social desirability and thin boundaries. Unpublished manuscript.

Ehrman, M., and R. Oxford. 1995. Cognition plus: correlates of language learning success. *The Modern Language Journal* 79:67–89.

Eliot, T. S. 1917. *Prufrock and Other Observations*. Egoist Press: London.

Ellenbogen, J. M., J. D. Payne, and R. Stickgold. 2006. The role of sleep in declarative memory consolidation: Passive, permissive, active or none? *Current Opinion in Neurobiology* 16:716–722.

Ellis, H. R. 1988. Dream drama: an effective use of dreams (part 2). *Dream Network Bulletin* 7:16–17, 19–20.

Federn, P. 1952. *Ego Psychology & the Psychoses*. New York: Basic Books.

Fisher, S., and S. Cleveland. 1968. *Body Image & Personality* (2nd ed.). New York: Dover.

Fiss, H., G. S. Klein, and E. Bokert. 1966. Waking fantasies following interruption of two types of sleep. *Archives of General Psychiatry* 14: 543–551.

Fiss, H. 1986. An empirical foundation for a self psychology of dreaming. *Journal of Mind and Behavior* 7:161–191.

Fookson, J., and J. Antrobus. 1992. A connectionist model of bizarre thought and imagery. In J. Antrobus, and M. Bertini (Eds.), *The Neuropsychology of Sleep and Dreaming*. Hillsdale, NJ: Lawrence Erlbaum Associates. pp. 197–214.

Foote, S. L., R. Freedman, and A. P. Oliver. 1975. Effects of putative neurotransmitters on neuronal activity in monkey auditory cortex. *Brain Research* 86:229–242.

Foulkes, D. 1966. *The Psychology of Sleep*. New York: Charles Scribner's Sons.

Foulkes, D. 1982. *Children's Dreams*. New York: Wiley.

Foulkes, D. 1999. *Children's Dreaming and the Development of Consciousness*. Cambridge, MA: Harvard University Press.

Foulkes, D., M. Hollifield, L. Bradley, R. Terry, and B. Sullivan. 1991. Waking self-understanding, REM-dream self representation, and cognitive ability variables at ages 5–8. *Dreaming* 1:41–52.

Foulkes, D., and G. Vogel. 1965. Mental activity of sleep onset. *Journal of Abnormal Psychology*, 70:231–243.

Freeman, W. J. 1999. *How Brains Make up their Minds*. London: Weidenfeld and Nicholson.

Freud, S. 1953 [1900]. *The Interpretation of Dreams*, standard edition, Vols. 4 and 5. London: Hogarth.

Funkhauser, A, O. Würmle, C. Cornu, and M. Bahro. 2001. Dream life & intrapsychic boundaries in the elderly. *Dreaming* 11:83–88.

Gackenbach, J. 1991. Frameworks for understanding lucid dreaming: a review. *Dreaming* 1:109–128.

Galvin, F. 1993. The effect of lucid dream training upon the frequency & severity of Nightmares. Unpublished Doctoral dissertation, Boston University.

Gelman, S. A., and E. M. Markman. 1986. Categories and induction in young children. *Cognition* 23:183–209.

Giambra, L., R. Jung, and A. Grodsky. 1996. Age changes in dream recall in adulthood. *Dreaming* 6:17–31.

Globus, G. 1993. Connecitonism and sleep. In Moffitt, A., M. Kramer, and R. Hoffman. (Eds.), *The Functions of Dreaming*. Albany, NY: State University of New York Press.

Greenberg, R. and C. Pearlman. 1975. A psychoanalytic dream continuum: The source and function of dreams. *The International Review of Psychoanalysis* 2:441–448.

Gregory, R. L. 1997. *Eye and Brain, 5th* ed. Princeton, NJ: Princeton University Press

Hall, C. S. 1947. Diagnosing personality by the analysis of dreams. *Journal of Abnormal and Social Psychology* 42:68–79.

Hall, C. S. 1953. *The Meaning of Dreams*. New York: Harper.

Hall, C. S. 1966. *The Content Analysis of Dreams*. New York: Appleton-Century-Crofts.

Hall, C. S. 1984. The ubiquitous sex difference in dreams, revisited. *Journal of Personality and Social Psychology* 46:1109–1117.

Hall, C. S. and W. G. Domhoff. 1963. A ubiquitous sex difference in dreams. *Journal of Abnormal & Social Psychology* 66:278–280.

Hall, C. S. and R. Van de Castle. 1966. *The Content Analysis of Dreams*. New York: Meredith.

Hallowell, A. 1966. The role of dreams in the Ojibwa culture. In G. Von Grunebaum and R. Caillois, (Eds.), *The Dream and Human Societies*. Berkeley, CA: University of California Press pp.267–289.

Harrison, R. H., E. Hartmann, and J. Bevis. 2005–2006. The Boundary Questionnaire: Its preliminary reliability and validity. *Imagination, Cognition, and Personality* 25:355–382.

Hartmann, E. 1965. The D-state: A review and discussion of studies on the physiological state concomitant with dreaming. *New England Journal of Medicine* 273:30–35, 87–92.

Hartmann, E. 1966. The psychophysiology of free will: An example of vertical research. In R. Lowenstein, L. Newman, M. Schur, and A. Solnit (Eds.), *Psychoanalysis, A General Psychology*. International Universities Press: New York. pp. 521–536.

Hartmann, E. 1967. *The Biology of Dreaming*. Springfield, Charles C. Thomas.

Hartmann, E. 1968. The 90-minute sleep-dream cycle. *Arch Gen Psychiatry* 18:280–286.

Hartmann, E. 1970. The D-state and norepinephrine-dependent systems. In E. Hartmann (Ed.), *Sleep and Dreaming*. Boston: Little, Brown & Co. pp. 308–328.

Hartmann, E. 1973. *The Functions of Sleep*. New Haven, CT: Yale University Press.

Hartmann, E. 1976. The dream as a "royal road" to the biology of the mental apparatus (Discussion of the changing use of dreams in psychoanalytic practice). *International Journal of Psychoanalysis* 57:331–334.

Hartmann, E. 1984. *The Nightmare: The Psychology and Biology of Terrifying Dreams*. New York: Basic Books.

Hartmann, E. 1988. Paper presented at a meeting: *The functions of sleep*. Winnipeg, Manitoba, Canada.

Hartmann, E. 1989. Boundaries of dreams, boundaries of dreamers: thin & thick boundaries as a new personality dimension. *Psychiatric Journal of the University of Ottawa* 14:557–560.

Hartmann, E. 1991. *Boundaries in the Mind*. New York: Basic Books.

Hartmann, E. 1991. Dreams that work or dreams that poison: What does dreaming do? *Dreaming* 1:23–25.

Hartmann, E. 1992. Boundaries in the mind: Boundary structure related to sleep and sleep disorders. *Sleep Research* 21:126.

Hartmann, E. 1995. Making Connections in a Safe Place: Is Dreaming Psychotherapy? *Dreaming* 5:213–228.

Hartmann, E. 1996. Outline for a theory on the nature and functions of dreaming. *Dreaming* 6:147–170.

Hartmann, E. 1998/2001. *Dreams and Nightmares: The New Theory on the Origin and Meaning of Dreams*. New York: Plenum Press. Revised paperback edition, 2001, New York: Perseus Books.

Hartmann, E. 1999. Dreaming Contextualizes Emotion: A New Theory on the Nature and Functions of Dreaming. In H. Bareuther, VK. Brede, M. Ebert-Saleh, K. Grünberg, S. Hau, (Eds.), *Traum, Affekt und Selbst*. Tübingen: Fuldaer Verlagsanstalt.

Hartmann, E. 1999. Dreams contextualize emotion: a new way of understanding dreams and dream symbolism. *Psychoanalytic Dialogues* 9: 779–788.

Hartmann, E. 2000. We do not dream of the 3 R's: Implications for the Nature of Dreaming Mentation. *Dreaming* 10:103–111.

Hartmann, E. 2007. The Nature and Functions of Dreaming. In D. Barrett and P. McNamara, (Eds.), *The New Science of Dreaming, Vol III*. Westport CT: Praeger. pp. 171–192.

Hartmann, E. 2008a. The central image (CI) makes "big" dreams big: the central image is the emotional heart of the dream. *Dreaming* 18:44–57.

Hartmann, E. 2008b. Dreaming: The Contemporary Theory. *The American Psychoanalyst* 42(3):10, 30–32.

Hartmann, E. 2010. *Boundaries: A New Way to Look at the World*. CIRCC, California.

Hartmann, E. and R. Basile. 2003. Dream imagery becomes more intense after 9/11/01. *Dreaming* 13:61–66.

Hartmann, E. and T. Brezler. 2008. A systematic change in dreams after 9/11/01. *Sleep* 31:213–218.

Hartmann, E., R. Elkin, and M. Garg. 1991. Personality & Dreaming: the dreams of people with very thick or very thin boundaries. *Dreaming* 1:311–324.

Hartmann, E., R. Harrison, J. Bevis, I. Hurwitz, A. Holevas, and H. Dawani. 1987. The Boundary Questionnaire: A measure of thin & thick boundaries derived from work with nightmare sufferers. *Sleep Research* 16:274.

Hartmann,E. and R. Kunzendorf. 2005–06. The Central Image (CI) in recent dreams, dreams that stand out, and earliest dreams: Relationship to boundaries. *Imagination, Cognition and Personality* 25:383–392.

Hartmann, E., and R. Kunzendorf. 2006–07. Boundaries and dreams. *Imagination, Cognition and Personality* 26:101–115.

Hartmann, E., R. Kunzendorf, A. Baddour, et al. 2002–2003. Emotion makes daydreams more dreamlike, more symbolic. *Imagination, Cognition, and Personality* 22:55–274.

Hartmann, E., R. Kunzendorf, R. Rosen, and N. Grace. 2001a. Contextualizing images in dreams and daydreams. *Dreaming* 11:97–104.

Hartmann, E., R. Rosen, N. Gazells, and H. Moulton, 1997. Contextualizing images in dreams images that picture of provide a context for an emotion. *Sleep Research* 26:274.

Hartmann, E., R. Rosen, and N. Grace. 1998. Contextualizing images in dreams: more frequent and more intense after trauma. *Sleep* 21S:284.

Hartmann, E., R. Rosen, and W. Rand. 1998. Personality and dreaming: Boundary structure and dreams. *Dreaming* 8:31–40.

Hartmann, E., and R. Stickgold. 2000. Contextualizing images in content obtained from different sleep and waking states. *Sleep* 23S:A172.

Hartmann, E., and M. Zborowski. 2001. Dreams: Correlates of the contextualizing image. *Sleep* 24S:A174.

Hartmann, E., M. Zborowski, and R. Kunzendorf. 2001b. The emotion pictured by a dream: An examination of emotions contextualized in dreams. *Sleep and Hypnosis* 3:33–43.

Hartmann, E., M. Zborowski, R. Rosen, and N. Grace. 2001c. Contextualizing images in dreams: More intense after abuse and trauma. *Dreaming* 11:115–126.

Hebb, D. O. 1949. *The Organization of Behavior: A Neuropsychological Theory*. New York: Wiley.

Herman, J. L. 1992. *Trauma and Recovery*. New York: Basic Books.

Hillman, D. J. 1990. The emergence of the grassroots dreamwork movement. In S. Krippner (Ed.) *Dreamtime & Dreamwork: Decoding the Language of the Night.* Los Angeles: Jeremy P. Tarcher, Inc. pp. 13–20.

Hobson, J. 1965. The effects of chronic brainstem legions on cortical and muscular activity during sleep and waking in the cat. *Electroencepholography and Clinical Neurophysiology* 19:41–62.

Hobson, J. A., R. W. McCarley, and P. W. Wyzinski. 1975. Sleep cycle oscillation: Reciprocal discharge by two brainstem neuronal groups. *Science* 189:55–58.

Hoppenbrouwers, T., J. C. Ugartechea, D. Combs, J. E. Hodgman, R. M. Harper, and M. B. Sterman. 1978. Studies of maternal-fetal interaction during the last trimester of pregnancy: Ontogenesis of the basic rest-activity cycle. *Experimental Neurology* 61:136–153.

Hunt, H. T. 1995. *On the Nature of Consciousness: Cognitive, Phenomenological and Transpersonal Perspectives*. New Haven: Yale University Press.

James, W. 1907. *Pragmatism: A New Name for Some Old Ways of Thinking.* New York: Washington Square Press, 1983.

Jones, R. 1962. *Ego Synthesis in Dreams*. Cambridge: Schenkman.

Jouvet, M. 1962a. Paradoxical sleep – a study of its nature and mechanisms. In K. Akert, C. Bally, & J. Schade (Eds.), *Sleep Mechanisms (Progress in Brain Research, Vol. 19)* Amsterdam: Elsevier. pp. 20–62.

Jouvet, M. 1962b. Recherches sur les structures nerveuses et les mécanismes responsables des différetnes phases du sommeil physiologique. *Arch Ital Biology* 100:125–206.

Jouvet, M. 1969. Biogenic amines and the states of sleep. *Science, 163*, 32–41.

Jung, 1965. *Memories, Dreams, Reflections.* Aniela Jaffe (Ed.) New York: Vintage.

Kandel, E. R. 2006. *In Search of Memory*. New York: Norton.

Kintsch, W. 2008. How the mind computes the meaning of metaphor: A simulation based on LSA. In R. W. Gibbs, Jr. (Ed.), *The Cambridge Handbook of Metaphor and Thought*. New York: Cambridge University Press. (pp. 129–142).

Klinger, E. 1990. *Daydreaming.* Los Angeles, CA: Tarcher (Putman).

Koulack, D. 1991. *To Catch A Dream: Explorations of Dreaming.* Albany: State University of New York.

Kozmová, M. and R. N. Wolman. 2006. Self-awareness in dreaming. *Dreaming* 16:196–214.

Kramer, M. 1993. The selective mood regulatory function of dreaming: An update and revision. In A. Moffit, M. Kramer, and R. Hoffman (Eds.), *The Functions of Dreaming.* Albany: State University of New York Press. pp. 139–196.

Krippner, S., I. Wickramasekera, J. Wickramasekera, and C. Winstead. 1998. The Ramtha phenomenon: Psychological, phenomenological, & geomagnetic data. *The Journal of the American Society for Psychical Research* 92:1–24.

Kunzendorf, R. 2007. Symbolic images in dreams and daydreams. In D. Barrett and P. McNamara (Eds.), *The New Science of Dreaming*. Praeger, Westport. Vol III, pp. 155–170.

Kunzendorf, R., E. Hartmann, R. Cohen, J. Cutler. 1997. Bizarreness of the dreams and daydreams reported by individuals with thin and thick boundaries. *Dreaming* 7:265–271.

Kunzendorf, R., E. Hartmann, L. Thomas, L. Berensen. 1999–2000. Emotionally directing visual sensations: I. Generating images that contextualize emotion and become "symbolic". *Imagination, Cognition and Personality* 19:269–278.

Kunzendorf, R., and J. Maurer. 1988–89. Hypnotic attenutation of the 'boundaries' between emotional, visual, & auditory sensations. *Imagination, Cognition & Personality* 8:225–234.

LaBar, K. S. and R. Cabeza. 2006. Cognitive neuroscience of emotional memory. *Nature Reviews: Neuroscience* 7:54–64.

LaBerge, S. 1985. *Lucid Dreaming*. New York: Ballantine.

LaBerge, S., L. Levitan, and W. C. Dement. 1986. Lucid dreaming: Physiological correlates of consciousness during REM sleep. *Journal of Mind and Behavior* 7:251–258.

Lakoff, G. 1993a. The Contemporary Theory of Metaphor. In A. Ortony (Ed.), *Metaphor and Thought*. Cambridge: Cambridge University Press.

Lakoff, G. 1993b. How metaphor structures dreams: the theory of conceptual metaphor applied to dream analysis. *Dreaming* 3:77–98.

Lakoff, G. and M. Johnson. 1980. *Metaphors We Live By*. Chicago: University of Chicago Press.

Lakoff, G. 2009. Index of Lakoff Metaphors. Retrieved April 21, 2009 from http://cogsci.berkeley.edu/lakoff/metaphors/

Landis, B. 1970. Ego boundaries. *Psychological Issues, 6,* Monograph #24. New York: International Universities Press.

Léna, I., S. Parrot, O. Deschaux, et al. 2005. Variations in the extracellular levels of dopamine, noradrenaline, glutamate, and aspartate across the sleep-wake cycle in the medial prefrontal cortex and nucleus accumbens of freely moving rats. *Journal of Neuroscience Research* 81:891–899.

Levin, R., G. Fireman, and C. Rackley. 2003. Personality and dream recall frequency: Still further negative findings. *Dreaming* 13:155–162.

Levin, R., J. Galen, and B. Zywiak. 1991. Nightmares, boundaries, and creativity. *Dreaming* 1:63–74.

Levin, R., L. Gilmartin, and L. Lamontanaro. 1998–99. Cognitive style and perception: the relationship of boundary thinness to visual-spatial processing in dreaming and waking thought. *Imagination, Cognition, and Personality* 18(1):25–41.

Lewin, K. 1936. *Principles of Topological Psychology*. New York: McGraw-Hill.

Maquet, P., J. Peters, J. Aerts, et al. 1996. Functional neuroanatomy of human rapid-eye movement sleep and dreaming. *Nature* 383: 163–166.

Maquet, P., P. Ruby, S. Schwartz, et al. 2004. Regional organization of brain activity during paradoxical sleep (PS). *Arch Ital Biology* 142: 413–419.

McCrae, R. 1994. Openness to experience: expanding the boundaries of factor V. *European Journal of Personality* 8:251–272.

Mellman, T. A., D. David, V. Bustamante, J. Torres, and A. Fins. 2001. Dreams in the acute aftermath of trauma and their relationship to PTSD. *Journal of Traumatic Stress* 14:241–247.

Modell, A. 2003. *Imagination and the Meaningful Brain*. Cambridge: MIT Press.

Moffitt, A., M. Kramer, and R. Hoffmann. (Eds.), 1993. *The Functions of Dreaming*. Albany: SUNY Press.

Morewedge, C. K., and M. I. Norton. 2009. When dreaming is believing: The (motivated) interpretation of dreams. *Journal of Personality and Social Psychology* 96:249–264.

Nofzinger, E. A., M. A. Mintun, M. B. Wiseman, and J. Kupfer. 1997. Forebrain activation during REM sleep: An FDG PET study. *Brain Research* 770:192–201.

Ozick, C. 1989. *Metaphor and Memory*. New York: Alfred A. Knopf.

Palombo, S. 1992. Connectivity and condensation in dreaming. *Journal of the American Psychoanalytic Association* 40:1139–1159.

Panksepp, J. 1998. *Affective Neuroscience: The Foundations of Human and Animal Emotions*. New York: Oxford University Press.

Payne, J. D., R. Stickgold, K. Swanberg, and E. A. Kensinger. 2008. Sleep preferentially enhances memory for emotional components of scenes. *Psychological Science* 19:781–788.

Perls, F. S., R. F. Hefferline, and P. Goodman. 1951. *Gestalt Therapy*. New York: Julian Press.

Poe, G. R., D. A. Nitz, B. L. McNaughton, and C. A. Barnes. 2000. Experience-dependent phase-reversal of hippocampal neuron firing during REM sleep. *Brain Research* 855:176–180.

Pujol, J. F., J. Mouret, M. Jouvet, and J. Glowinski. 1968. Increased turnover of cerebral norepinephrine during rebound of paradoxical sleep in the rat. *Science* 159:112–114.

Punämaki, R. L. 1999. The relationship of dream content and changes in daytime mood in traumatized vs. non-traumatized children. *Dreaming* 9:213–233.

Punämaki, R. L. 2007. Trauma and dreaming: Trauma impact on dream recall, content, and patterns, and the mental health function of dreams. In D. Barrett and P. McNamara (Eds.), *The New Science of Dreaming: Volume 2*. Praeger: Westport, Connecticut. pp. 211–251.

Purcell, S., J. Mullington, A. Moffitt, R. Hoffman, and R. Pigeau. 1986. Dream self reflectiveness as a learned cognitive skill. *Sleep* 9:423–37.

Qin, Y. L., B. L. McNaughton, W. E. Skaggs, and C. A. Barnes. 1997. Memory reprocessing in corticocortical and hippocampocortical neuronal ensembles. *Philosophical Transactions of the Royal Society of London. Series B: Biological Sciences* 352:1525–1533.

Rader, C., R. Kunzendorf, and C. Carrabino. 1996. The relation of imagery vividness, absorption, reality boundaries and synesthesia to hypnotic states and traits. In: R. Kunzendorf, N. Spanos, and B. Wallace (Eds.), *Hypnosis and Imagination*. New York: Baywood Publishing Company. pp. 99–121.

Rados, R., and R. D. Cartwright. 1982. Where do dreams come from? A comparison of presleep and REM sleep thematic content. *Journal of Abnormal Psychology* 91:433–436.

Roussy, F., C. Camirand, D. Foulkes, J. De Koninck, M. Loftis, and N. Kerr, N. 1996. Does early-night REM dream content reliably reflect presleep state of mind? *Dreaming* 6:121–130.

Rapaport, D. 1952. The conceptual model of psychoanalysis. In D. Krech and G. S. Klein (Eds.), *Theoretical Models and Personality Theory*. Durham, NC: Duke University Press, pp. 56–81.

Rapaport, D., M. Gill, and R. Schafer. 1945/1946. *Diagnostic Psychological Testing* (2 vols.). Chicago: YearBook.

Rechtschaffen, A. 1978. The single-mindedness and isolation of dreams. *Sleep* 1:97–109.

Rechtschaffen, A., B. M. Bergmann, C. Eveson, C. Kushida, and M. Gilliland. 1989. Sleep deprivation in the rat. X. Integration and discussion of the findings. *Sleep* 12:68–87.

Rechtschaffen, A., M. A. Gilliland, B. M. Bergmann, and J. B. Winter. 1983. Physiological correlates of prolonged sleep deprivation in rats. *Science* 221:182–184.

Reinsel, R., J. Antrobus, and M. Wollman. 1992. Bizarreness in dreams and waking fantasy. In J. Antrobus and M. Bertini (Eds.), *The Neuropsychology of Sleep and Dreaming*. Hillsdale, NJ: Lawrence Erlbaum Associates pp. 157–183.

Reiser, M. 1997. The art and science of dream interpretation: Isakower revisited. *Journal of the American Psychoanalytic Association* 45:891–905.

Reiser, M. 1990. *Memory in the Mind and Brain: What Dream Imagery Reveals*. New York: Basic Books.

Resnick, J., R. Stickgold, C. D. Rittenhouse, and J. A. Hobson. 1994. Self representation and bizarreness in children's dream reports collected in the home setting. *Consciousness and Cognition* 3:30–45.

Revonsuo, A. 2000. The reinterpretation of dreams: An evolutionary hypothesis of the function of dreaming. *Behavioral and Brain Sciences* 23: 877–901.

Robbins, P., and F. Houshi. 1983. Some observations on recurrent dreams. *Bulletin of the Menninger Clinic* 47:262–265.

Robert, G., and A. Zadra. 2008. Measuring nightmare and bad dream frequency. Impact of retrospective and prospective instruments. *Journal of Sleep Research* 17:132–139.

Roffwarg, H. P., J. N. Muzio, and W. C. Dement. 1966. Ontogenetic development of the human sleep-dream cycle. *Science* 152:604–619.

Rumelhart, D. E., and J. L. McClelland. 1986. On learning the past tenses of verbs. In J. L. McClelland, D. E. Rumelhart, and PDP Research Group (Eds.), *Parallel Distributed Processing, Vol. 2, Psychological and Biological Models*. Cambridge, MA: MIT Press.

Ryan, C. 2000. Personality of fashion models. (Unpublished Master's thesis, Saybrook Graduate School, San Francisco).

Sand, S. and R. Levin. 1996. Concordance between Hartmann's Boundary Questionnaire and the Eysenck Personality Inventory. *Perceptual and Motor Skills* 82:192–194.

Schredl, M. 2008. Review of the dream experience: A systematic exploration. *Dreaming* 18:280–286.

Schredl, M. 2007. Dream recall: models and empirical data. In D. Barrett and P. McNamara (Eds.), *The New Science of Dreaming: Volume 2*. Praeger: Westport, Connecticut. pp. 79–114.

Schredl, M. 1995. Traumerinnerung: Persönlichkeitsdimension oder von situativen Faktoren beeinflußt? *Psychologische Beitrage, 37*, 133–180.

Schredl, M., P. Kleinferchner, and T. Gell. 1996. Dreaming and personality: Thick vs thin boundaries. *Dreaming* 6:219–223.

Schredl, M. and A. Montasser. 1996. Dream recall: State or trait variable? Part I: Model, theories, methodology and trait factors. *Imagination, Cognition, and Personality* 16:181–210.

Schredl, M., and E. Piel. 2003. Gender differences in dream recall: Data from four representative German samples. *Personality and Individual Differences* 35:1185–1189.

Schredl, M., G. Schäfer, F. Hoffmann, and S. Jacob. 1999. Dream content and personality: Thick vs. thin boundaries. *Dreaming* 9:257–263.

Siegel, A. 1996. Dreams of firestorm survivors. In D. Barrett (Ed.), *Trauma and Dreams*. Cambridge, MA: Harvard University Press.

Singer, J. 1988. Sampling ongoing consciousness and emotional experience: implications for health. In: M. J. Horowitz (Ed.), *Psychodynamics and Cognition*. Chicago: University of Chicago Press. pp. 297–346.

Singer, J. 1993. Experimental studies of ongoing conscious experience. In *Experimental and Theoretical Studies of Consciousness*. NY: Wiley and Sons. pp. 100–116.

Smith, C. 2010. Sleep states, memory processing, and dreams. *Sleep Medicine Clinics* 5:217–228.

Snyder, F. 1965. The organismic state associated with dreaming. In N. Greenfield & W. Lewis (Eds.), *Psycho-analysis and Current Biological Thought*. Madison, WI: University of Wisconsin Press. pp. 275–315.

Snyder, F. 1970. The phenomenology of dreaming. In L. Madow and L. Snow (Eds.), *The Psychodynamic Implications of the Physiological Studies on Dreams*. Springfield, IL: Thomas. pp. 124–151.

Solms, M. 1997. *The Neuropsychology of Dreams*. Mahwah, NJ: Lawrence Erlbaum Associates.

Strauch, I., and B. Meier. 2004. *Den Träumen auf der Spur: Zugang zur modernen Traumforschung*. Bern: Verlag Hans Huber.

Stewart, D. W., and D. Koulack. 1993. The function of dreams in adaptation to stress over time. *Dreaming* 3:259–268.

Stickgold, R., L. Scott, C. Rittenhouse, and J. A. Hobson. 1999. Sleep induced changes in associative memory. *Journal of Cognitive Neuroscience* 11:182–193.

Stickgold, R. 2005. Sleep-dependent memory consolidation. *Nature* 437: 1272–1278.

Strauch, I. and S. Lederbogen. 1999. The home dreams and waking fantasies of boys and girls between ages 9 and 15. *Dreaming* 9:153–161.

Strunz, F. 2003. Preconscious mental activity and scientific problem-solving: A critique of the Kekule dream controversy. *Dreaming* 3:281–294.

Sutton, J., H. Breiter, J. Caplan, et al. 1996. Human brain activation during REM sleep detected by fMRI. *Neuroscience Abstracts* 22:690.

Suzuki, H., M. Uchiyama, H. Tagay, et al. 2004. Dreaming during non-rapid eye movement sleep in the absence of prior rapid eye movement sleep. *Sleep: Journal of Sleep and Sleep Disorders Research* 27:1486–1490.

Stevenson, R. L. 1892. *Across the Plains*. Leipzig: Bernhard Tauchnitz, 211–232.

Stickgold, R., L. Scott, et al. 1999. Sleep induced changes in associative memory. *Journal of Cognitive Neuroscience* 11:182–193.

Sullivan, K. 1998. *Recurring Dreams*. San Francisco: Crossing.

Ullman, M. 1959. The adaptive significance of the dream. *Journal of Nervous and Mental Disease* 129:144–149.

Ullman, M. 1969. Dreaming as metaphor in motion. *Archives of General Psychiatry* 21:696–703.

Ullman, M. 1988. The experiential dream group. In M. Ulman & C. Limmer (Eds.), *The Variety of Dream Experience: Expanding Our Ways of Working with Dreams*. New York: Continuum.

Ullman, M. 2006. *Appreciating Dreams: A Group Approach*. New York: Cosimo.

van der Kolk, B. A. 1997. The psychobiology of posttraumatic stress disorder. *Journal of Clinical Psychiatry* 58:16–24.

Wagner, U., S. Gais, and J. Born. 2001. Emotional memory formation is enhanced across sleep intervals with high amounts of rapid eye movement sleep. *Learning & Memory* 8:112–119.

Walker, M. P. and R. Stickgold. 2006. Sleep, memory, and plasticity. *Annual Review of Psychology* 57:139–166.

Walpole, H. 1906 [1764]. *The Letters of Horace Walpole* [complete set] 1st edition. Peter Cunningham (Ed.) Edinburg.

Wamsley, E. J. and J. S. Antrobus. Dream production: A neural network attractor, dual rhythm regional cortical activation, homeostatic model. In D. Barrett and P. McNamara (Eds.), *The New Science of Dreaming: Volume 1*. Westport, CT: Praeger. pp. 155–184.

Wilson, M. A. and B. L. McNaughton. 1994. Reactivation of hippocampal ensemble memories during sleep. *Science* 265:676–679.

Wikipedia: The Free Encyclopedia. (2008, November). FL: Wikimedia Foundation, Inc. Retrieved April 21, 2009 from http://en.wikipedia.org/wiki/Metaphor

Wingert, C. and M. Kramer. 1979. *Dimensions of Dreams*. Gainesville, FL: University Presses of Florida.

Woodward, D., H. Moises, B. Waterhouse, B. Hoffer, and R. Freedman. 1979. Modulatory action of norepinephrine in the central nervous system. *Federation Proceedings* 38:2109–2116.

Worsley, P. 1988. Personal experiences in lucid dreaming. In J. Gackenbach and S. LaBerge (Eds.), *Conscious Mind, Sleeping Brain: Perspectives on Lucid Dreaming*. New York: Plenum. pp. 321–342.

Yamanaka, T., Y. Morita, and J. Matsumoto. 1982. Analysis of the dream contents in Japanese college students by REM-awakening technique. *Folia Psychiatrica et Neurologica Japonica* 36:33–52.

Yu, C. K. 2006. Brain mechanisms of dreaming. (Doctoral Dissertation, University of Cape Town, South Africa, 2006).

Zborowski, M., E. Hartmann, M. Newsom, and M. Banar. 2003–2004. The Hartmann Boundary Questionnaire: Two studies examining personality correlates and interpersonal behavior. *Imagination, Cognition, and Personality* 23:45–62.

Zborowski, M., P. McNamara, E. Hartmann, M. Murphy, and L. Mattle. 1998. Boundary structure related to sleep measures and to dream content. *Sleep* 21S:284.

Zwig, A. 1990. A body-oriented approach to dreamwork. In S. Krippner (Ed.), *Dreamtime & Dreamwork: Decoding the Language of the Night*. Los Angeles: Jeremy P. Tarcher, Inc. pp. 78–86.

Author Index

Subject Index

Note: Page numbers followed by "*f*" and "*t*" refer to figures and tables, respectively.